IMAGINING A
NEW CHURCH

Cover Photo Description

This is the Passion Façade of the Sagrada Familia, also known as the Expiatory Temple of the Sagrada Família. It is located in Barcelona, Spain. The construction for this Temple began in 1882 for the purpose of honoring the "Holy Family." Antoni Gaudi, a devout Catholic and the inspiration behind Catalan Modernism, took over as chief architect in 1883. The Temple, dedicated by Pope Benedict in 2010 as a Basilica, is still under construction. It's anticipated completion is set for 2026, 100 years after the untimely death of Gaudi, the designer and true inspirer of this creation. The Sagrada Familia is considered one of the most unique and unlikely designs created for a church. It is something never before imagined. It seems the perfect metaphor to inspire the imagination of a new church for the 21st century.

Passion Façade   Interior   Nativity Facade

www.sagradafamilia.org

IMAGINING A
NEW CHURCH

What if We're Asking the Wrong Questions?

JEFFREY KJELLBERG

WESTBOW
P R E S S®
A DIVISION OF THOMAS NELSON
& ZONDERVAN

WestBow Press books may be ordered through booksellers or by contacting:

WestBow Press
A Division of Thomas Nelson & Zondervan
1663 Liberty Drive
Bloomington, IN 47403
www.westbowpress.com
1 (866) 928-1240

ISBN: 978-1-9736-6970-8 (sc)
ISBN: 978-1-9736-6969-2 (hc)
ISBN: 978-1-9736-6971-5 (e)

Library of Congress Control Number: 2019910526

Print information available on the last page.

WestBow Press rev. date: 09/11/2019

ACKNOWLEDGEMENTS

This book would never have been possible without the inspired assistance of my editor Michele Rubin. She was everything I couldn't have been in the process of writing the manuscript. I am also indebted to Lauren Tarshis, who introduced me to the talents of Michele. My wife Melanie was an essential partner in making sure my sentence structures were crafted correctly with precise punctuation. Thank you to my consulting partners that I'm blessed to lead at both Kairos and The Joshua Group who encouraged me every step of the way to get this book published. Finally, I need to thank all my friends and colleagues who took the time to read snippets of my book, giving me the assurance that I have a voice to share.

WHAT PEOPLE ARE SAYING

"As a respected and innovative leader, Jeffrey Kjellberg has repeatedly proven himself as one who can spark and sustain the fullness of a holy imagination. We are fortunate to receive his voice and vision, especially in times such as these, for he challenges us to resist our fears, receive amazing grace and embrace inconvenient questions in order to flourish as participants in God's ongoing mission. As one who has received an assortment of insights through his teaching, I recommend *"Imagining a New Church"* for all those seeking to serve with an inquisitive mind, courageous spirit, and burning heart."

Rev. Dr. Brian E. Konkol
Dean of Hendricks Chapel, Syracuse University

" 'What if...?' It's one of most powerful questions in our language because it invites us to challenge the status quo and see new possibilities. Drawing upon years of experience as a pastor, business strategist, and church consult, Jeffrey Kjellberg uses a series of 'what if...?' questions to interrogate our assumptions about what congregational life should be, offers new possibilities for mission and ministry, and invites us to discover our holy purpose. Reading it will change the way you look at your ministry, your church, and possibly even your faith."

Rev. Dr. David Lose, Senior Pastor
Mt. Olivet Lutheran Church, Minneapolis, MN

"The questions and insights raised in *"Imagining a New Church"* stretches our conversations and assumptions to prepare for a journey into the future that will require courage, collaboration, resilience, joy and hope for the generations to come. Jeffrey Kjellberg brings insight, as well as challenge, to engage church leaders in welcoming the struggles and the discernment of the Spirit needed for renewing our proclamation and purpose for a new day."

Rev. Claire S. Burkat
Retired Bishop of the Southeastern Pennsylvania Synod of the ELCA

"What do you do when you find yourself impossibly stuck? That is a difficult question for any individual; it is an even harder question for an organization. For more than a generation, the Church has found itself impossibly stuck, mired by a set of basic assumptions that stopped working in the 1960's. Jeffrey Kjellberg has found a solution, namely, asking different questions. In each chapter he invites the reader to explore a radically new "What If" question. And no matter how you personally resolve each one, these questions are worthy of being asked and answered. It just may lead the Church into a new future."

Dr. Steven Goodwin
Owner/Consultant, TurningWest, Inc.

Dedicated to the Love of My Life

My wife, Melanie Kjellberg, has been the force and support behind most of my professional career. It was her confidence in me that led to my decision to leave the security of parish ministry and become a consultant. It was her trust in my abilities that led to my purchasing of Kairos and the starting of two additional consulting firms. She never questioned the risks and challenges that come with these decisions. All she said was, "I have no doubt you can do this." So far, so good!

CONTENTS

CHAPTER 1

What If...?

W HEN I WAS YOUNG, MY PARENTS CALLED me "the inquisitive one." I always wanted to explore, experience, and discover what was around me. I wanted to open every box and see what was inside. I began every conversation with a question. Asking 'why' informed how I looked at the world. One of my favorite expressions was 'what if'? My father was a pastor, and although he wasn't necessarily the most patient man in the world, his ministerial work had taught him to be more patient than was his natural inclination. He would try to answer my 'what ifs' and accommodate my endless pestering, until one day he snapped, "what if this, what if that, that's all you can say is what if. There is no such thing as what if!" My father, who was a sensitive and kind man, had just shut me down. He didn't try to engage me, or deflect me. He had been worn out by my endless probing and speculating – to the point of ending the conversation.

I have never forgotten him saying that. It hurt, and frankly, I didn't believe him. What do you mean, there is no such thing as 'what if'? The world was filled with 'what ifs'! As I grew up, I found myself asking 'what if' a lot. I realized this question was woven into the fabric of what inspires our lives. This question is at the very heart of progress and change. It exposes us to the possible – what is and what could be. Asking 'what if' enables us to pause and take the time to wonder and appreciate. It also can help us unsettle ourselves – push ourselves beyond what we think we know as we ponder answers.

Yes, there is such a thing as 'what if'. And because there is, inspired things happen. 'What if' pushes the envelope and forces us to think beyond our current boundaries. It creates the space essential to wondering, listening, and exploring. Contemplating 'what if' can move us into new experiences. It helps us envision ways to see how the impossible can become possible.

Asking Hard Questions

Being involved with the church has always been a part of my life. As a child, I grew up as a PK (Pastor's Kid). Our family was at the church at least two or three times a week for events, activities, potluck suppers, and so much more. It was our way of life. As an adult, church remained the center of my life. I was an advisor for national youth gatherings and became an ordained minister. I was a pastor for both small and large congregations, eventually leaving the parish to be a church consultant. Now, I direct three different consulting companies that serve faith-based communities in a variety of ways. My entire life is embedded in church culture and the way of faith.

The church of my youth was the church of the 50's, 60's and early 70's. At that time, the church was experiencing unprecedented growth. It seemed current and engaged; influencing culture with relevant broad-based impact around the country. It was providing thought leadership, and our youth groups were strong and vibrant. Well attended Bible Camps were popping up all over the country. Creative missional initiatives were common place. Resources were available – both human resources and financial resources. We were encouraged to step out, take risks, and be experimental. Faith communities were being planted in newly organized towns and in city developments. To me, this was a church I wanted to be a part of. I saw it making a difference in my life and in the lives of so many around the world. It was impressive. I didn't necessarily know why this was happening or what was driving this movement. I was just inspired by it and that inspiration led me to my choice of career.

Then, something happened. I had joined the church community to be part of this forward-moving momentum. But instead of experiencing that energy, I began to see and feel something different. I sensed fear, anxiety, and deep uncertainty. I had committed to a church that had invigorated spiritual energy – a place where people were eager to raise their hands to get involved. But now I encountered a church that was tired and filled with self-pity. There was no longer a sense of vitality or an eagerness to figure out what we should do next. Instead, people were preoccupied with 'how do we keep this going?' People were no longer showing up looking to participate and get involved. Priorities were changing. The value of making the church a significant part of one's life was dissolving at stunning rates. And, most alarming of all, nobody had a clue as to why this shift was happening.

There were folks who thought knew why. Quick fix answers were flying around like wildfire. Books about church growth became must-read material and were on pastors' bookshelves everywhere. Starting a contemporary worship service was touted as the ideal solution in bringing back young people. Removing denominational identity from church names was a sure thing to attract the unchurched, de-churched or whatever churched they might be. Entertainment evangelism became a catch phrase. Doing teaching sermons was showing up in preaching seminars around the country. The list of 'solutions' went on and on. There were endless ideas and actions that promised to answer and reverse the reality of decline and impending irrelevance. It isn't that any one of these ideas were bad ideas. They just fell into the category of being reactive answers to a much deeper phenomenon that was happening.

I have a friend who travels around the country giving presentations to church leaders on a number of topics, mostly relating to how the church might imagine itself into the future. One of the things he often says is, "The church is in decline, but it isn't your fault." I have great respect for my friend, and I know he is trying to instill hope instead of despair. But I find myself disagreeing with him on this. As hard as it is to watch the decline happening in our churches across the country, shifting blame to others or factors out of our control doesn't serve us all that well. I don't believe there have been intentional efforts from faith community leaders to sabotage the church as we know it. If that has happened, it isn't through malice or intent. I also believe that we are being buffeted by some realities that are indeed beyond our control. We have not intentionally created our own problems.

But in order to fully respond to the challenges facing us, we need to look at ourselves without timidity or defensiveness. There is tremendous benefit in taking a step back and asking ourselves how we may have contributed to this decline. Asking ourselves where we may have played a role in our own situation can shift us from helplessness to empowerment. Trying to figure out how to change something we have no power to change is debilitating. But digging into what we do have control over is encouraging. Finding how we can play a part in our own transformation is exhilarating and vitalizing.

What do we possibly have to lose by doing this? It would be difficult to make things worse. Are we afraid of what we might discover? We might make ourselves uncomfortable or find that we have to move outside our frame of reference. We might find it all too threatening or too scary. We might realize that we ourselves need a radical type of change. Instead of looking at the people who have stopped showing up (or never came in the first place), we need to look at ourselves. We can't look for people outside our community to figure it out for us.

The decline of our church has left us feeling diminished, and has left our leaders feeling depressed and helpless. It has pushed them out of the ministry and has discouraged others from ever thinking about becoming a church leader. It has created all kinds of fearful and reactive thinking and behavior. But we can't be held hostage to failure and resign from reality. Instead, we must look at a changing world with open eyes and an open spirit. We must confront our fears and anxieties and transform from within.

I decided to write this book because I believe there is a different way to approach this challenge. Instead of trying to fix the problem or wallowing in despair over what has been lost, we must focus on going deeper and ask difficult and disruptive questions. We need to put everything on the table that has defined us as church for the past decades and centuries. There are things we can learn about who we have been and why we have behaved the way we have. We can learn from what we have said and what we have or haven't done. We cannot separate ourselves from what is happening in our church, but it is not a hopeless situation. God hasn't left the arena. Taking deliberate steps to be more in tune with what God is up to might just bring a powerful re-imagining for the church's future.

Asking 'what if' is my way of beginning this process. I want to invite us into the hard questions. Only the hard questions will bring us to a place of deeper self-discovery and an acknowledgment of what we can and can't control. My whole life has been blessed by moments when I asked 'what if' instead of resigning myself and thinking 'this is hopeless'. Those 'what if' moments often helped me see what I might have gotten wrong. Those moments helped me shift my behavior and change my response. Those moments led me to new action. It helped me change. This moment in time is pivotal for faith community leaders and it calls us to find a new way. We know that we can have impact and bring fresh meaning to communities. We have traditionally been meaning-makers in an uncertain world. But we need to look at how we got where we are and understand where we lost our way forward. We need to do this without envy and without fear. The world doesn't need ministries that have thrown in the towel. Instead, the world needs faith communities to dive into this moment with open minds and hearts believing there is important work still to be done.

CHAPTER 2

What If Truth is Color Blind?

I HAPPEN TO BE COLOR BLIND. MY CHILDREN always thought this meant I just needed better glasses. But the term color blindness is a bit of a misnomer. It isn't a form of blindness as such – it is a kind of deficiency in the way one sees, or rather perceives, color. My form of color blindness allows me to see the basic colors. My deficiency is in not being able to see the whole spectrum of colors that exist. I am fortunate. Many of my relatives are also color blind but have a much more severe case, allowing them to only see the grayscale of color.

What I have discovered about colorblindness is fascinating. It is mostly found in men (1:12) and more rarely in women (1:255). The cause of color blindness occurs in the X chromosome. When it is present, a deficiency happens in the three different color cones of the retina (Red, Green, Blue). Either one of the three doesn't work, is missing all together, or all three are deficient. Most men have XY chromosomes. Women are mostly XX. This gives them an exponentially better chance of having at least one of their X chromosomes without the carrier of color blindness. Consequently, they have a much less chance of being colorblind. In addition, because women most often are XX, if neither of those X's is a colorblind carrier, they can potentially see even more colors than the average human. It is believed that non-colorblind people can see up to 1 million different color hues. For women who have both X chromosomes be non-colorblind carriers, 2-3% of them can see up to 16 times more colors than the average person. No wonder women and men don't always see "eye to eye."

I have also discovered that it is not only an X chromosome deficiency that can affect one's ability to see colors. Our cultural and environmental circumstances can also influence the colors we see. There was a famous color study conducted with the Himba tribe in Namibia. The Himba are a semi-nomadic, pastoralist and indigenous people living in the northern part of the country. They are the last semi-nomadic people in Namibia. The Himba are distinctive for a number of reasons, but one is that they have had no Western cultural influences on their way of life. Because of this, they were a perfect group to work with in studying how people recognize colors. The focus of the study was to determine if language and culture influenced one's ability to recognize colors. The study was conducted with Himba who spoke no other languages other than their own language of OtjiHimba.

The study's intent was to see if the way the Himba categorized color influenced the colors they perceived. Western culture languages use eleven color categories - green, blue, yellow, red, white and so forth, while the Himba use four. During the study, the Himba were given a collection of twelve colored tiles arranged in a circle – eleven were the same color and one different. They were asked to choose the one that looked different from the others. The initial test was

this miracle of life. Our response to this yearning has been to work to understand the meaning of the universe, the purpose of life, and the powers at play in our midst. The work to understand is, in and of itself, both powerful and empowering. The difficulty has always come when these myriad perspectives, or multiple lenses to life, become the one true lens.

For Christendom, this happened quite early in its development, even prior to Constantine declaring it as the religion of the empire. The specific purpose of the New Testament's early writers was to begin framing a particular perspective of God and this person Jesus. Matthew, Mark, Luke and John all had unique lenses to share their understanding of God's truth. In addition, there were early interpreters of these witnesses that struggled with just exactly who Jesus was: human only, God AND Human, spirit only, etc. Even within the first 300 years of Christianity, there was an emerging orthodoxy as well as what would be seen as heresy. Fissures formed that developed into differentiated schools of thought and belief systems – with each claiming that they possessed the right way of knowing the truth.

For Martin Luther, this notion of exclusivity held by the few for the many was a significant part of his effort to reform the institutional church. He had witnessed the church's misuses of power and authority. He had seen it controlling access to education and the interpretation of the scriptures. And he was convinced this needed to change. Luther's methodology was based in the principle that he could bring his teachings directly to the people. However, it was unquestionably based on the belief that his own knowledge – his own truth – was a testament to the real truth. In his writing of the small catechism, designed to help church leaders uniformly teach the true faith, he states after each explanation to the three articles of the Apostle's Creed, "This is most certainly true." There was no ambiguity for Luther. He believed fully that what he was claiming was the truth of God, a truth he dedicated his entire life to teaching, preaching, and witnessing.

Much of the institutional church that evolved out of this reformation movement formed around the model of right knowing. The myriad of denominations that evolved crafted their own unique doctrines and confessional statements that created clear edges for what was "right" and what was "wrong" for the believer to claim. The majority of these denominations organized in such a way that allowed them to control and administer their brand of truth. Preaching was the cornerstone of worship. It was where you were told how to rightly understand scripture and accept the teachings of the one true faith (a one true faith which every denomination claims to have). Schools for faith education were created for children, youth, and adults. Church buildings were designed to reflect this core value to rightly teach the faith. In fact, much of the church that we have experienced over the last several centuries closely followed this educational structure. Superintendents, teachers, classroom helpers, students, the pastor's study, etc. – all were embedded within this over-arching design. The church was even successful in getting a weekday dedicated to their educational endeavors.

So why does this matter? What can we learn from this intersection of belief and power? Where does the question "what if truth isn't meant to be owned" live within this history?

Existentially speaking, God has been present from the beginning of time, long before humans ever showed up in the mix. Just because we have the innate propensity to define, and subsequently confine, the reality of God, it doesn't mean God is limited. God was, and is, far more than what we have the capacity to articulate. To behave as though it is only within the last several millennia that 'God' has become God, limits the experience of God's truth. It limits us. Our current living reality doesn't lend itself to this type of thinking. We are an expanded, multigenerational culture these days. From Boomers to Generation Xers, to Millennials, Centennials, and onward, there is a much greater level of tolerance and complexity around the world's diversity. This is especially true as it relates to self-awareness and an understanding of God. It extends outward to one's world view, and how we define our purpose and meaning for life.

The world, at its best, is a place where this kind of wonder and exploration occurs and is encouraged. But for both wonder and exploration to thrive, we need to create the kind of space that allows for it. We must have a space where mystery can be mystery, uncertainty can be uncertainty, and where glimpses of the whole are allowed to be glimpses. This doesn't mean abandoning our core values and fundamental belief systems. Uncertainty is not equal to disavowal. Rather, it is a call for us to move away from being tellers and owners of truth to becoming a people who invite others into the experience and wonder of *our glimpse* of the truth. Not our ownership of the whole of truth, but our experience of the flash of our truth.

So, what if truth isn't owned, can't be owned? Rather than see this question as destabilizing, let us see it as liberating. When we begin to wonder how truth can bless and invite, not limit or exclude, we free ourselves from the constraints of rigidity. We are open to what others experience as spiritual truth. This does not weaken nor negate our own. It enlarges our sense of God and enlarges our role in the world. There also is a freedom that comes when we don't use our truth to delegitimize anyone else's experience of truth. If God is bigger than our ability to define, or confine, then what we are really trying to do is simply get the best glimpse, flash, encounter, experience, that we can. To truly know God is to simply love God. To love the light that God desires for us. This creates an incredible amount of space to wonder and experience the presence of God.

Which brings me back to my metaphor of being colorblind. The fullness of the color spectrum exists no matter how one sees it or even if one sees it. The millions of color hues are at play and are real. Just because a colorblind person has a particular glimpse of one kind of color and another person can see exponentially more color, one vision doesn't delegitimize the other. Both have had an experience of color's reality. If we can truly become a culture that celebrates one's glimpses of truth, then I think we will have a much greater chance to broaden our ability to impact and bless others. We will be acquiring the tools we need to survive in an endlessly complicated and changing world.

CHAPTER 3

What if Religion is Inclusive?

I HAD THE PRIVILEGE OF TRAVELING TO Zimbabwe the summer after I graduated from college. Zimbabwe (formerly known as Rhodesia) had secured its freedom from apartheid rule and the oppressive regime of Ian Smith. I traveled with a number of North American college students, sponsored by the Lutheran World Federation (LWF). We were to learn about the LWF's work in Africa, and bring the story of their mission and its impact back to churches in the United States. It was a truly transformational moment in my faith journey, and in the evolution of my world view.

We lived in a remote village outside of the capital city of Harare for six weeks, developing relationships, and listening to the stories of Zimbabwe's struggle for freedom. We observed just how LWF was trying to equip the Zimbabwean people to reclaim their country with success. We weren't quite sure what to expect when we were asked to take this journey. Most of us weren't totally familiar with what LWF was doing in Africa – this was why it was important for us to go in the first place. Was it a mission field designed to convert the natives to Christian beliefs? Was it a rebuilding effort to help Zimbabwe recover from years of war and struggle? Was it both? We just didn't know.

To our joy and surprise, we quickly learned that this LWF mission post in Kuwadzana, Zimbabwe was a newly formed co-operative, the purpose being to help teach skills to women and men that could be utilized in the country's rebuilding efforts. Some of the men in this co-operative had been taken from their homes when they were just ten years old to fight in the bush for freedom. They were now in their 20's. They had fought for their country's liberation from colonialism, but those years of war had left them with little or no training in the basic labor skills necessary for success in their now-new country. What LWF was doing was incredible. They were getting in the trenches with these women and ex-combatants, nurturing them with love and helping to equip them with necessary skills. We were inspired to be a part of this enterprise.

One of the great benefits of living in the co-operative was developing deep relationships. We heard heart-breaking stories of war and oppression alongside litanies of joy and celebration. The violence and fear that Zimbabwe had lived with was being transformed into freedom and hope. We sang together around the fire, drank horrific beer made from fermented corn meal, and walked in the bush hand in hand. We shopped the markets and broke bread together. It was life changing and life giving.

I'll never forget the day I was walking hand in hand with Roger, one of the ex-combatants living in the co-operative. We had become friends and developed a trusting relationship. I was flattered that he chose to hold my hand when we walked because that was a sign of a deeper relationship and trust. When you hold another's hand in this culture, it means you are giving yourself fully to the conversation.

I wish we had that tradition in the United States. While we were walking out in the bush, Roger pointed to the beautiful hills that just popped out of the ground. They were striking in their formations. It reminded me of the Black Hills of South Dakota. He explained that those hills were the resting places of his ancestors. They were places of great honor that housed the wisdom and spirit of those who had gone before. They were sacred places that were given tremendous respect. He shared some of those ancestor's legacies with me, and talked about the wisdom they continued to share with his people. It was obvious to me that those hills were critically important to his faith and life journey.

Then, he shared with me a story that broke my heart. He said, "When I was young, we had missionaries that came to us and told us that we had to stop honoring these hills and our ancestors that rested there. We were told this was the work of evil spirits and went against God's will. Our hearts ached when they told us this." I was dumbfounded and ashamed. I had an uncle who served as one of these missionaries, and I knew this was part of his message. I let the conversation hover in silence for quite some time, not really knowing what to say. I found it incredibly painful that, as part of the goals of a missionary's work, was to strip someone of their own history and erase a source of their strength. In that silence, I experienced the gulf between intention and consequence. Then, I simply squeezed Roger's hand and said, "I am sorry that happened. I hope you know that we respect your belief and want to honor your ancestors."

What if religion is a gift and not a command? What if it is not a mandate? What if the way in which we have chosen to articulate our understanding of God is a way to bless us, not restrict us? As I mentioned in the previous chapter, every form of religious expression has claimed to be the one true faith - the one truth that is the holder of truth. But I want us to open ourselves up to a new possibility. We are living in a world of globalization – of knowledge, faith, and culture. What might we do to let this be seen as a gift instead of seeing it as a potential threat?

My friend Roger had a very deep connection with his ancestors, their wisdom, faith and encouragement, which was manifested in the mountains; mountains that had surrounded him every day of his life. What benefit was there in stripping that from his very being? What if those missionaries had instead seen his beliefs as a gift and blessing to his life? How did stripping a loving belief from a people give witness to the missionaries' certitude of a loving and compassionate God? Instead, what if the missionaries had opened themselves to the possibility that there was something to be learned in the way Roger's people honored the wisdom and legacy of their ancestor? Perhaps learning about it could have blessed those early missionaries.

There are so many religious expressions of faith that could be classified as blessings, rather than restrictions that exclude. Claiming one expression as our own shouldn't restrict us from having and experiencing other expressions. I was struck by the beauty of that thought a number of years ago when watching a television show.

Northern Exposure was a must watched show in the early 90's. Situated in the remote fictional town of Cicely, Alaska, the show used a very eclectic cast of characters to bring about unique and comedic life lessons. A young and snarky Jewish doctor from New York, a former astronaut turned obnoxious millionaire businessman, a debutante from Detroit turned bush pilot, an aged bar owner who married a stunning former beauty pageant winner who was 40 years his junior, an ex-convict turned local disc jockey, and so on. It was always enjoyable, but often deeply philosophic. One such episode that has always stood out to me was titled "Kaddish For Uncle Manny."

Joel was the Jewish doctor from New York. He was a recent graduate from medical school, sent to Cicely to repay a school loan that was funded by Alaska. He was obviously a fish out of water in this very-back-woods community. A northern bush town in Alaska, needless to say, had no Jews living there. As the title of the episode indicates, the main plot was about Joel's challenge of needing to say Kaddish – the Mourner's Prayer for the Dead - for his deceased Uncle Manny. According to Jewish tradition, the family of the deceased must recite the Kaddish prayer as part of the ritual of mourning and remembrance. Reciting the Kaddish is one of the most important acts of faith for a Jew. Tradition states that this must be done in the presence of at least 10 other Jews, called a minyan.

That was Joel's problem. Where was he going to find a minyan in Cicely to gather for him to say Kaddish? The episode was in season four, so Joel had had plenty of time to develop relationships amongst the misfits of Cicely. At first, these friends committed to searching the countryside for any Jew they could find, offering them a small fee to come sit with Joel while he said the Kaddish. As the recruitment drama unfolded, Joel became increasingly frustrated with the idea that he would be saying Kaddish with 10 complete strangers. Not only did that not seem right to the character, it also seemed antithetical to the purpose of the ritual. His Uncle Manny was like a father to him. Saying Kaddish was a very personal act to be shared with other mourners. Hired Jews didn't seem to fit the purpose of the prayer.

After a few days of the search process, Joel finally said, "enough!" It was more important for him to say Kaddish with people he cared about, rather than complete strangers - regardless of their particular religious leanings. So, he asked his friends if they would join him in saying the Kaddish, and to do so in a way that reflected their own tradition of honoring the dead.

The final scene of the episode was powerful. Joel stood in front of the gathered congregation, wearing the necessary attire to fulfill Jewish requirements - his yarmulke and prayer shawl that were gifts from his Uncle Manny. The congregation was his community. These were the people who cared for him and whom he cared for, eclectic and eccentric as they may be. As he began to say the Kaddish, each friend responded in a way that honored not only Joel's tradition and his uncle, but their own, as well. Some bowed their head, some raised their hands, some knelt, some stood. In that moment, the religious practice became blessing to all who were participating. Most importantly, mourning the loss of Uncle Manny was allowed to happen. In joining together and honoring all traditions, the community was strengthened and the presence of God affirmed.

Sadly, at the writing of this chapter, there was a mass murder at The Tree of Life Synagogue in Pittsburgh, PA, the largest mass killing of Jews in our nation's history. It was horrifying to hear the words of the murderer spewing anti-Semitic hatred during his arrest. For the country, it was one of our lowest moments as a nation. We have not unlearned hatred. However, there was a response to this outrage that contained both beauty and blessing. Faith communities around the country acted in solidarity with this Synagogue. Christians, Jews, Muslims and other faith expressions shared their love and support. They gathered for Shabbat the week after the murders to pray for those who were killed, their families and the country as a whole. It was the epitome of seeing religion as blessing for the sake of God's people.

I grew up in a very diverse family as it related to Christian belief. I had what would be called the far right, literalist conservatives on one side and the progressive liberals committed to social justice and religious freedom on the other. To say the least, it made for very interesting family gatherings. Sometimes, it would lead to harsh and hurtful conversations, occasionally leaving some in tears. One was right, the other wrong, even to the point of being damned to hell. These moments left a very deep scar on my faith journey. How can this be what God is wanting from us? Are we really meant to have all the answers based on certainty and right thinking? Are we really meant to condemn – or even just dismiss - others who experience the presence and power of God differently than ourselves?

We had a very poignant moment during a Thanksgiving meal at my Aunt and Uncle's home. We were going around the table, sharing what we were thankful for, when one of my liberal-leaning family members shared their hope for justice for the LGBTQ culture, and for those suffering from severe poverty in India. At that point, my right-leaning uncle weighed in and said, "You know, God is punishing the LGBTQ culture with AIDS because of their sinful behavior, and the people of India are impoverished because they have rejected Jesus as their Savior." Needless to say, this was one of those moments where dialogue led to tears, and eventually the end of our gathering.

It is a struggle for me to believe that God has instilled in us the ability to craft religious beliefs and practices in order to reject, hurt, and even condemn others to death. If it is true that the way in which we can know God is to love God, then I believe this dialectic trumps any of our humanly-crafted convictions or actions that fly in the face of that love.

There are a number of ideas about the etymology of the word "religion". As with most word formations, they are developed out of experiences or discoveries that call for some form of definition or articulation. Some historians believe its origins go back to the 12th Century and are related to describing, or defining, monastic cultures. Others say "religion" doesn't really exist. Jonathan Z. Smith states, "religion is solely the creation of the scholar's study. It is created for the scholar's analytic purposes by his imaginative acts of comparison and generalization. Religion has no existence apart from the academy" (Jonathan Z. Smith in Imagining Religion). It seems that one doesn't go far enough and the other goes a bit overboard. Somewhere in between is the theory that "religion" is from the Latin word "religare." Religare has a connotation of being bound to another, most specifically, of humans having a bond to God. What I appreciate about this explanation is that it doesn't provide specific criterion for a belief system. Rather, it simply defines the condition that this word reflects – that human beings are bound to God.

If we are truly bound to God, and God is love, what does that ultimately mean? Can we interpret loving as knowing? What if that is the ultimate gift of religion, to love and know simultaneously?

This is not as radical as it might seem. As children of God, there is a fundamental affirmation that we are loved by God. Thus, as children of this loving God, we have an intrinsic call to love. We believe that, in our love for each other, we are also reflecting God's love for us. In doing so we express a knowing that mirrors God. If this is true, why should God's children only be able to love God in one way and through one belief? Surely God's love is unending enough – and our ability to love expansive enough – to encompass this.

The consequence of this belief is that it compels us to begin whittling away at many religious presuppositions. These are the suppositions that have "bound" us to ways of behaving and believing that exclude rather than include all people. As we reflect on what we may have done to contribute to the dwindling impact and relevance of faith communities in this 21st Century, we need to look at ourselves first. We tend to look at the outside world – its differences and diversities - and blame 'change' for our loss. But when we look at our own practices and professions, we may see that our expectations of our religious behavior don't need to be rigid and prescribed. In fact, we can see that our faith is always leading us to new ways of being and behaving. Faith is never static. It is always expanding, shifting, growing, changing and renewing itself. And this is never something to fear but is something to be embraced and celebrated. The 21st Century is well upon us and we cannot turn back the clock.

CHAPTER 4

What if our Why isn't the Why We Thought it Was?"

THE QUESTION OF 'WHY' HAS BECOME A crucial one in church culture. It can sound practically self-explanatory – we are here because we are a people of faith – but it is much more complex than that. Two consulting companies I lead take this question very seriously because it has significant value in helping faith community leaders focus on the very purpose of their organization's existence. In the 1990's, the big push was in claiming your "mission, vision and values." This had a fairly significant impact, buy ultimately failed in addressing the deeper issues behind the mission. Mission was more synonymous with what the church was doing rather than understanding why it was doing it. Every community is unique, every culture is different, and every moment in time calls for new and reimagined ways of thinking and behaving. Knowing your 'why' in the midst of this is essential. Simply doing what you have always done, but trying to just do it better is often self-defeating. Not knowing why you have been doing what you are doing inhibits your community's ability to forge a fresh path forward.

When we ask ourselves why we are who we are, we take an important first step in unpacking the purpose of our community. It is always easy for us to assert our missional agendas and practices as exemplars of our behavior. But when we ask ourselves why we do what we do, things become more complicated and difficult.

I recently worked in a congregation where this challenge was becoming debilitating for their leadership. This congregation had known tremendous success in the late 20th Century, but its impact and membership engagement had been dwindling for the past several decades. When I work with a congregation, the first thing I put in place is a deep listening process. I conduct an online assessment that my consulting company designed to measure the overall health and effectiveness of the church's missional culture. I then spend time doing more intimate listening and learning with one-on-one and group sessions. It's the classic model of quantitative and qualitative data gathering. I believe this is critical in gaining perspective and understanding the unique circumstances of each community.

What I learned about this particular congregation during this process was very telling. The members showed a deep longing for the congregation to once again be that primary influence within the community that it had been for many years. But they no longer had any real clarity about their missional purpose or identity. They knew what they wanted to be, but had no idea why. This disconnect isn't unique to this one congregation. It is a real epidemic in most faith communities around the country. They long for what was, and are literally stuck in that longing. They have no idea why they need to move forward into a new missional future. More troubling is that they can't really articulate why they did what they were doing in that past. This confluence of issues literally stymies their ability to see what might be. For this particular culture, it was at a crisis level. They believed that they could rely on their past to again become a key player in their community. The problem was they had no understanding of why they should do this, let alone how.

Coming out of our deep listening exercises, I recommended that they undertake a missional renewal process. This involves revisiting their 'why'- what I call their holy purpose – and clarifying that holy purpose in response to their current reality and potential. This is where things began to break down. As I challenged them to try and answer what their holy purpose had been for their mission and ministry, they could only reference what they did through their programs. "We have great music and worship. We have a dynamic youth program. We have done great things for the community with our recovery program." This was all wonderful, but had nothing to do with their holy purpose. I kept pushing them to try and define this – what was their purpose behind their ministry practices? They struggled, got frustrated and began to displace their frustration back on me. It wasn't that they didn't know the answer to what I was asking - they didn't understand it. I kept saying, "You are telling me how you do things, not why you do them." They weren't able to separate the how from the why – the two felt like one and the same to them and they were deeply frustrated.

After a few intense sessions, I decided to take a deeper dive with them into their holy purpose. For example, having a dynamic youth ministry isn't a holy purpose, it's a program and a practice. I decided to approach the issue differently. I asked them, "Why do you prioritize your ministry around youth? Why do you invest in providing exceptional music and worship experiences? Why is having a recovery program so vital to your missional DNA?" I asked straightforward questions that would hopefully spark a different way of answering. As they began to wrestle with this, lightbulbs started turning on. The youth program in and of itself wasn't their holy purpose. The fact that there were youth in the community that needed a place to be cared for, loved, given alternative ways of understanding themselves, freed from homelessness and drug addiction, and so much more, was really what laid behind their actions. Now, they could start to see behind the practice (what & how) and start to make some deeper connections to what moved them into these practices.

They started to see a theme emerge. Their holy purpose wasn't for the sake of simply doing things - there was a greater intention behind those actions. In the end, they arrived at a truly new understanding of who they were: "Our community needs a light to shine in the midst of the darkness and challenges that we all face." Their holy purpose slowly emerged from just engaging in their standard behavior to being driven by this intense desire "To Be A Light." It isn't necessarily very complicated, but it is very purpose-driven. It connected their sense of identity to their actions. Their 'why' – their holy purpose – was in being a light to the community. That in and of itself is revelatory.

It's hard, trying to really connect to the "why" behind our actions. What is the motivating or defining factor that calls us to behave the way we do? This is our holy purpose as people of faith. It's there. But we don't always know how to name it, and it isn't necessarily what we really think it is.

The Evolution of Christendom's Why

In the very beginnings of Christianity, there was no institutional influence that shaped it's holy purpose. There were the beginnings of Christological understandings, but nothing was controlled by a larger institutional body (that would emerge later). What did exist was a simple collection of converts following "The Way", which they believed Jesus had called them into living. The earliest glimpses of this comes from both New Testament writings and early church historians. Paul wrote in Philippians 2: 1-5, "If then there is any encouragement in Christ, any consolation from love, any sharing in the Spirit, any compassion and sympathy, make my joy complete: be of the same mind, having the same love, being in full accord and of one mind. Do nothing from selfish ambition or conceit, but in humility regard others as better than yourselves. Let each of you look not to your own interests, but to the interests of others. Let the same mind be in you that was in Christ Jesus..." The holy purpose – or the 'why'- of this early faith community known as "The Way" was to have and be the mind of Christ in community. It wasn't based on any particular theological mandates. Rather, it was a very simple alignment of their sense of meaning and purpose with that of what they saw in the person of Jesus. Their way of being was their holy purpose.

An early Christian historian and convert, the North African Tertullian, who lived from around 160-225 AD, wrote this about his newfound faith community: "We are a body knit together as such by a common religious profession, by unity of discipline, and by the bond of a common hope...But it is mainly the deeds of a love so noble that lead many to put a brand upon us. See, they say, how they love one another."*

In his research on the rise of early Christianity, Sociologist Rodney Stark summarizes the early Christians this way, "Christianity served as a revitalization movement that arose in response to the

---

* From the Apology of Tertullian, AD 197

Biblical narrative, stripping it from the very people for whom it was intended. Lost in our somewhat colloquial understanding of Luther was that his intention was NOT to start a new church movement. His goal was to bring the one true church back to where he believed it was intended to be - in the hands of all God's faithful people.

In spite of these intentions, a new church movement was exactly what happened - and not just one, but many. There were a number of reformers and they each developed faithful followers. Many became the pillars of this 'protestant' initiative. Lutherans, Calvinists, Methodists, Anglicans, Congregationalists, etc., all emerged out of this reforming time. But, instead of this movement calling the church back to its original understanding of its holy purpose - to be followers of "The Way" - it developed a very differently focused missional objective. This seismic shift was moving the church to a different form of power and control - defending the right way to believe. Because the church had deviated so far from what was understood to be its original purpose, the new reformers were determined to encapsulate the right way to believe and live as God's followers. It was, if you will, a kind of over-correction.

Luther was prolific in his writings and avid in his response to this wave of reformation. As mentioned in chapter two, he wanted to bring what he understood as the real truth of the Gospel to the ordinary person. He wrote numerous treaties, books, instructional manuals, and articles describing the right way to believe. He wrote for pastors, parents, political authorities, and the common folks so they could see for themselves what they were being asked to believe. He advanced what was, to him, the real truth. All of this was done with the best of intentions. Luther wanted to free people from the manipulation and corruption that he saw from church authorities. Unfortunately, this didn't result in greater unity. Instead, it began a tidal-wave of division and balkanization among the emerging church leaders. The church's leaders shifted from what had previously been their center of gravity – power and control – to a new place of power and authority. Now, these church leaders asserted that they alone understood the right way to know and experience God. Each proclaimed itself as the one holder of God's truth, the one true way to believe.

This can be seen in nearly every aspect that developed out of the Reformation. Denominations became synonymous with right thinking and believing. To be Lutheran meant you believed in a very particular way. To be a Baptist you believed in a different way. Each denomination claimed to be right and believed the others were wrong. Division became normative, as more and more silos of expression developed. ELCA, LCA, ALC, AELC, LCMS, LCMC, WELS, NALC are just a small sampling of what has evolved in just the Lutheran expression. Literally hundreds of denominational identities have formed since the 1517 moment of posting those 95 Theses.

This is the church 'why' that we have inherited. It is an institutionally driven movement that primarily exists around drawing people into your particular way of believing and thinking. It's core purpose still is influenced by this need to teach, tell and inform people of correct thinking. Asserting its ownership of God's truth has become its holy purpose. Surely there has been much good that has happened from nearly all of these denominational and institutional expressions. However, it has created an environment of right and wrong, in and out, believer and non-believer, isolation and silos. Us and them. The divisions are entrenched, and collaboration around "The Way" has been negligible.

500 years after the great Reformation, we find ourselves once again in a major seismic shift in Christendom. As I mentioned in chapter two, our ability to claim that we have the one and only way

to experience and embrace the God of the universe is over. I would add that perhaps this should have never been part of our spiritual foundation. We are in a time that clearly calls us to reexamine our spiritual history and our holy purpose. We must seriously ask ourselves what is our holy purpose as faith communities? How are we being invited in this time to be the way of Christ, to embody the presence and power of the God we believe exists?

These questions are an invitation to faith communities to engage in a meaningful reflection of what underlies their actions and ways of doing ministry. We have lived out of a paradigm that expects us to be places of right teaching and right believing. We have buildings that were designed around this basic purpose. Seminaries still invest a significant amount of their curriculum around training teachers and preachers to advance the institutional understandings of scripture and theological rightness. None of this is done with ill intention. But it relies on a musty foundation that has outlived its usefulness. We are no longer asking ourselves the right questions.

So, what are we to do? As with any major systemic shift, our response calls for radical rethinking and a genuine realignment with the very bedrock of our being. If we continue to act in a way that believes our very purpose is to tell, teach, and inform people to believe in the one true way of faith, then we will be left behind. Emerging generations are not interested in being told how to believe, act or feel. They are more interested in being invited into an experience, or a genuine action, that allows them to encounter a greater good and larger purpose.

Now, suffice it to say, for the church to effectively evolve, it needs to examine its holy purpose; its 'why'. I will address some ways to dig into this in a later chapter but want to caution that this book is not intended to be prescriptive. Instead, it is intended to provoke conversation and serious dialogue amongst faith community leaders. It is to help them encounter new and effective strategies that re-embrace the original notion of "The Way": Being the mind of Christ; that accepts unconditionally, loves radically, and judges not. Stay tuned.

CHAPTER 5

What if We are Called to Collaborate?

I WAS FORTUNATE IN MY FIRST JOB, A CALL to be an associate pastor in a suburban community in the Twin Cities and paid me enough to afford a home. It didn't hurt that home prices weren't as insane as they are in many of today's markets. Truthfully, it was both invigorating and debilitating. Becoming a homeowner brought excitement, but trying to find a home that fit my expectations and pocket book was overwhelming.

In the process of looking for a home, the realtor brought me to a fairly new development on the edge of the community where I was going to be serving. As we drove into the development, the homes looked fairly decent, modest in size and each having a fairly large yard. Most were split entries, which was an unfortunate design concept in the 1980's. My realtor planned on showing me three or four homes. We stopped at the first one and took a look around the separate floors. There wasn't anything special about them, as they were in the "affordable" range for new home buyers. When we got to the top level of the home, the realtor took me outside to see the deck and the backyard. As I walked out of the home my heart sank. There was this maze of chain linked fences as far as the eye could see. Every house in this development had a fenced in back yard. No trees, no shrubs, just dozens of squared off grass areas with no interconnection.

I couldn't believe it. Why would anyone want to live in a neighborhood where everyone was isolated from each other by fencing? I can appreciate wanting to have a dog running around in your backyard, however, this development had taken that to a whole new level. I had never seen anything like it in my life, and I had lived in a number of communities growing up. Needless to say, we never made it to the other homes the realtor planned for me to see as I said, "I cannot imagine living in a place like this." It embodied the idea of disconnection and disunity. It was designed to isolate neighbor from neighbor and not create community.

What if we are called to collaborate, not isolate?

One of the hardest experiences I had serving as a parish pastor was the profound lack of meaningful collaboration and cooperation, not just amongst my own tribe of the Evangelical Lutheran Church in America (ELCA) congregations, but amongst any of the varied faith communities in the areas where I served. It felt very much like that housing development; everyone isolated and protecting their little plot of real estate.

My second call, still in the greater Twin Cities area, had a fairly long standing tradition of collaborating with a large Catholic church in the community. Within that collaboration there were six and eight congregations that had connected together to support and sustain a clothing and food shelf ministry, which operated out of this Catholic church. It had been quite successful and a decently cooperative partnership.

One day, I walked into the Catholic church for a planning meeting with this group. As I entered our meeting room, the two women from that church, who had been participating in this good work for many years, were in tears. I looked at both of them and asked what was wrong. They said together, "We have been told by our new priest that we are no longer allowed to be involved in any ecumenical partnerships. We have to end our work with this ministry." I couldn't believe what I was hearing. Moreover, my heart ached for these two women who couldn't understand why this had to be. They had invested so much into this endeavor. They had no idea what could possibly be wrong in working together with other people in the community who shared similar passions and simply participated in different church cultures. To them, it made no sense.

I have mentioned in the last few chapters that the historical narrative of Christendom has too often been one of right and wrong, in and out, believer and non-believer. This has not just been at the feet of Protestants and the Catholic church. Most faith expressions have their variation of this propensity to hold others in judgement and isolate themselves instead of collaborate.

But, what if we are called to collaborate, not isolate?

As mentioned, my own tribe is not immune to this kind of impulse. I grew up as a PK (Pastor's Kid) in what was then the American Lutheran Church (ALC). I was ordained into the newly formed ELCA. Both of these Lutheran bodies were the result of mergers bringing together Lutheran denominations that developed separately from each other, mostly because of ethnic connections and sometimes theological differences. There were German Lutherans, Swedish Lutherans, Norwegian Lutherans, Finish Lutherans, etc. Currently, in the ELCA, there are a little over 9,000 congregations that make up the denomination, many of which still hold to some of that ethnic and former denominational heritage. That isn't all bad - except when it becomes an absolute barrier to collaborate or join together in more impactful and effective ways.

Let me share two classic examples of this inability to join together. There is a town in Minnesota that has a one square block park in the heart of the city. Surrounding this park in each direction are four Lutheran churches, three of which are ELCA, the other is a Wisconsin Evangelical Lutheran Synod (WELS) congregation. From this park, you can literally see all four of these churches. The ELCA has been in existence for over 30 years and still these three congregations remain completely separated in their identities clinging to their heritage that preceded the ELCA merger in 1988. It isn't for me to throw judgement at these churches as to why they have stayed separate entities. It simply causes one to scratch their head and ask, "how does operating three separate facilities, staffs, and ministry plans make sense when you share the same denominational identity and practically the same address? I am not sure how much collaboration happens among these three entities. I do know they all have a shared desire to stay isolated and separate from each other on many levels.

The second example, and perhaps less obvious, is a suburban area in a major city in the Midwest. In this suburb, which encompasses about a 15 square mile area, there are eight ELCA Lutheran congregations, not to mention four other Lutheran congregations with other denominational identities. These ELCA churches aren't across the street from each other but each are within a few minutes drive. From the epicenter of this community you can be at any one of those eight congregations within ten minutes. During the 30 plus years that these congregations have shared the same denominational identity, there has been little to no discussion of how they could be better together verses separate and isolated. None of them want to consider giving up some of their past identity in order to discover a new way of being church in that community.

From my vantage point, wouldn't there be wisdom in seeing the power that might come in joining together? Why cling to isolation? What if they brought all of their resources and capacities into a shared collaborative effort to do even greater work to impact the lives of the people in that community and far beyond? What is getting in the way of such action? Is it a fear of loss, losing control, compromising their identities? What if we dared to imagine something new, and perhaps risky and courageous, in being the church of the 21st century? Isn't it possible that coming together through collaboration could bring about a better, more impactful, way of being the people of God in the world today?

I believe that if we don't take this question seriously, we will suffer even more decline. I think we could dilute our ability as faith communities to love and care for the whole of God's creation even more. By continuing to claim our's is the only way, our truth is the whole truth, our practice is the right practice, then walls will continue to be in place. We don't always do this with clear intention. Much of it is a result of heritage, practice and teaching. We fall back on our history and our tradition because it's often easier. It goes back to the "why" question. Is it our purpose to be protectors of the truth, tellers of the right way to believe and behave, etc? Or, could it be that truth isn't owned, but experienced in small and meaningful ways? Is it possible that religious practice is not meant to serve as mandate but blessing to those who practice it? Could the why of our faith communities be about living into "The Way" of being the mind of Christ, loving, welcoming and acting for the sake of all?

These questions shouldn't be isolated to just Christian faith communities, even though that seems to be quite difficult in and of itself. This collaborative movement needs to be equally about an effort to see ourselves in shared mission with other faith expressions, not just the Christian way of being.

I am not a fan of inter-faith dialogue. I understand its purpose, but to merely talk amongst each other doesn't go far enough. We need to move this idea further down the road and see it as inter-faith collaboration and impact, collectively trying to change the world for the sake of all people. If God is bigger than religion, bigger than any framework we can craft, and has existed from the beginning of all time, isn't it plausible that God is at work in all things, including others' way of being faithful to this God?

Just imagine what could happen if we could break down those barriers of isolation and discover a way to work together, seeing the power of God at work in all we do.

Several years ago, my wife and I went to visit our daughter who was studying in Segovia, Spain for a semester. Like good parents, we felt it was our parental duty to go check on our daughter while overseas, and of course, take in a few sights along the way. One of those incredible sights was the region of Andalusia, specifically Seville. We had some knowledge of Spain and it's more recent history, mostly from what our daughter had shared with us. What we didn't know was the rich history that unfolded in Andalusia over a millennium ago.

From the late 9th century to around the time just before the reformation, there was somewhat of a cultural phenomenon happening in this little southern region of the Iberian Peninsula. At the time it was known as Al-Andalus and was under Muslim rule. One term used to describe this era is "la convivencia" or "the coexistence". Another term was "the Golden Age". What made it unique is that there was a convergence of the three Abrahamic religions living side by side in this small region of the world. Jews had arrived there soon after the diaspora when the Romans had overthrown Judea (1st century). Christians entered the scene around the time of the Edict of Milan (4th century). The Muslims showed up very shortly after the emergence of Muhammed and Islamic expansion (8th century). As each new political and religious power moved in, those that were there stayed. In the 9th century the region was under the control of the Muslims.

The intriguing outcome of this period was the forming of collaborative efforts in literature, art, and architecture. Some historians say this period is too romanticized in how collaborative it was. However, what we discovered in our visit was inspired evidence of how these religious and political cultures came together and created breathtaking works of art, palaces, and writings.

What I found to be so significant about this Golden Age wasn't that they saw themselves as being partners in a shared missional narrative. They still adhered to their own unique expressions and practices of their faith. What was inspiring is that they found a way to respect each other in their differences to the point of doing things together, not always in isolation or opposition. It's important to note that this period was in the heart of medieval times where one's life could be under serious threat, depending upon what religious identity you had. People were not being asked to consider becoming Muslim or Christian. They were given the option of doing so or getting killed if they didn't. To be in a place where coexistence was not only possible, but provided opportunity to collaborate, was unthinkable. Yet, in some small and not so small ways, this happened.

One of the more inspired outcomes of this collaborative time is the art of Flamenco dancing. In recent years this form of dancing has been influenced by many different cultures, and so what you see as Flamenco dancing isn't necessarily the form it was centuries ago. However, it is believed that as this artistic expression evolved it was influenced by all three of the major religious cultures that existed in the Andalusia region from the 8th – 14th century. When the Gypsy (Roma) culture arrived in the region in the 14th century they were quickly attracted to the art form that was developing. Out of this period came the melding of traditions to eventually create what is now called "Old World Flamenco" dancing. This purist form of the dance is quite inspired and when experienced the pain, struggle and joy of the cultures that influenced its style can easily be felt. The city of Madrid, Spain is home to some of the best artists still performing in this style.

In our current world environment, we hear so much rhetoric that pits religion against religion. The far right Christians, the radical left, Jihadists, conservative Jewish Orthodoxy to name a few. Much of the rhetoric is driven by the most extreme versions of these groups. It doesn't serve any real value in deepening one's appreciation for what really defines another's core values and purposes. In my research on the la convivencia, I came upon this reflection from Karen Armstrong, an accomplished author in comparative religions.

"In [the] early days, Muslims did not see Islam as a new, exclusive religion but as a continuation of the primordial faith of the, 'People of the Book', the Jews and Christians. In one remarkable passage, God insists that Muslims must accept indiscriminately the revelations of every single one of God's messengers: Abraham, Isaac, Ishmael, Jacob, Moses, Jesus, and all the other prophets. The Qur'an is simply a 'confirmation' of the previous scriptures. Nobody must be forced to accept Islam, because . . . God was not the exclusive property of any one tradition: the divine light could not be confined to a single lamp, belonged neither to the East nor to the West, but enlightened all human beings. Muslims must speak courteously to the People of the Book, debate with them only in 'the most kindly manner,' remember that they worshipped the same God, and not engage in pointless, aggressive disputes."

Obviously, this wasn't the full practice engaged as Islam expanded its reach. The same can be said for Christendom. However, what it reflects is a core desire to be in relationship, not isolation, of other religious expressions and cultures.

So, what happens if we are called to collaborate and not isolate?

My dream for the future of the church is that there is a movement that starts to examine how we are "in common" and not "in contrast". The beauty in this reforming of our imagination is that we could begin to realize that we don't have to fight to protect our territory, or what we believe is right. We can be freed from believing that it is our way or no way. Instead, we can be blessed by embracing faith practices as gift and not as a way to define who is in or out. What if we were free to experience a neighbor who is practicing their faith by saying prayers five times a day and celebrate how that provides deep meaning to their life and experience of God? And what if we were able to come together in our practices and do something collaboratively that could help expose the power of God's unconditional love for all? It may be a naive hope, but it is one I believe is getting nudged down the road by the world around us. There are new and beautiful expressions waiting to be shaped by a world of collaboration, not isolation. Perhaps there is a new kind of dance that will evolve from the many faith cultures that live together in community.

CHAPTER 6

What if Who You
ARE is Enough?

I HAVE GROWN UP ALWAYS BELIEVING THAT
I am both a Swede and a Norwegian. My last name is Kjellberg
after all, which is as Swedish and Norwegian as you can get. It was
never really proven to me that this was my DNA heritage, but I
believed my great-grandmother and my grandparents' stories of the
Old Country. They would talk about all the places that they had
lived or visited. My great grandmother would share her riveting
story of taking a ship as a little girl from Sweden to America. They
carried their traditions with them to this new country, and those
traditions have been carried on in me. We have Swedish meatballs at
Christmas – although NO LUTEFISK EVER – as well as pickled
herring and oyster stew, and we make lefse every year. We have Dala
horses, Norwegian plates and sweaters, rosemaling and Swedish
glassware. We say "skol" and actually look into each person's eyes

when doing so! We have adopted a great deal of our Scandinavian heritage and take great pleasure in keeping these traditions alive.

My wife and I were very amused when we traveled to Sweden and Norway a few years ago to visit my wife's distant relatives. We discovered that many of those traditions which we have imbedded in our own family life are no longer being practiced by the Swedes and Norwegians themselves. When we asked them, "How do you make lefse?" they just smiled at us and said, "we don't." Obviously, for them it isn't the Old Country, it is the 21st century and life has evolved like it has for the rest of us. Regardless, my whole life has been lived with the strong sense of being a full-blooded Scandinavian.

I recently had a visit with my dermatologist. While I was with my doctor I asked her to examine my hands. They were forming these odd growths in my palms. Looking at them, she immediately said, "oh, that's Vikings Disease." "Vikings Disease?" I asked. She explained that this is a condition that shows up in anyone whose bloodline is traced back to the Vikings. It was a condition that they had and it shows up wherever the Vikings left their footprint. After she shared this, I fist pumped and said "Yes, it's true, I really am a Viking!" I had always been proud of my lineage, but had never really had concrete proof. Now I did.

The 21st Century seems to have awakened our desires to know our genetic and ethnic origins. Of course, it is only recently that the average person has been able to access easy DNA testing. Companies like 23 and Me, and Ancestry have taken off. I can't tell you the number of people I have talked with who received a gift package from one of these testing companies as a birthday or Christmas gift. We are endlessly curious about our heritage and our personal family history. We know that each of us carries a story that is uniquely our own, passed down to us from our ancestors and the lives they lived.

And there can be surprises when we find out. We may have believed that we were only one thing, and come from one place, but our DNA will tell us a different story. Instead of being 100% Irish, we find that we are 67% Irish, 17% Iberian Peninsula, 12% Finnish and 4% Germanic. We can even discover that we are Neanderthals, and not as an insult. We find long-lost relatives and are able to fill in lost pieces of our own history.

But why do we care so much about parsing our own identities in this way? Because knowing who we are matters. It enhances our understanding of ourselves and answers questions that we might not even know we had. Really knowing and understanding our identity creates a sense of comfort and confidence in us. It allows us to look at ourselves with less fear. What has contributed to our nature? What makes us be the way we are? Why do we look, think, and behave in the ways we do? What should we anticipate for our future based on what we know about our past? These are all important questions and having the answers makes a difference.

But despite the surge in mail-order DNA testing, the desire to know who we are isn't a new phenomenon. It goes back to the very beginnings of our human existence. The ancient Hebrew text, The Psalmist, asks it outright; "When I look at your heavens, the work of your fingers, the moon and the stars that you have established; what are human beings that you are mindful of them...?" (Psalm 8:3-4). Since the beginning of our ability to wonder, we have shown the need to define, or capture, who we really are. It matters.

This had been one of my biggest frustrations in my lifetime experience of the Christian church. Instead of the church helping us be affirmed in who we are, all too often it has worked hard to let us know who we are not. Church always starts with "all are welcome," but it can quickly transform into "but actually only those who fit into this nice box that we have created." How is it possible to say "all are welcome" and then follow that up with criteria for what that means? You are welcome here, but only if you understand that you need to become something different than what you currently are. You are welcome here but only if you believe, think, live, and act as we do.

This approach applies to a wide range of behavior. You can't be too liberal in your thinking. You can't be too conservative. If you are living in a same sex marriage, then you will need to rethink your place here. If you believe that infants shouldn't be baptized, or adults only should take communion, then you probably shouldn't come back. No ex-felons or homeless people on our campus. The list can go on and on depending on how the church has subtly and not so subtly established what qualifies you to be accepted within its gates. It constantly reinforces its vision of who you must be and who you must not be if you want to be one of us.

But it isn't just about how the church has established certain qualifiers for who is really welcome. In order for the church to inculcate a sense of dependency from its flock, it must also present itself as the cure for those who don't conform. The hymns and litanies tell you that you are a wretch, weak, lost, sinful and unclean - incapable of navigating this journey as you are. You are automatically 'less than' and the church is here to fix that. I had a church client whose pastor stood every Sunday morning in front of the congregation and said, "Welcome Saints (pause) Welcome Sinners!" As I sat there and looked around at who was listening, I thought, "if I was a visitor new to this faith journey, what in the world would that say to me? How is this in any way an 'all are welcome' culture?" Is the mission of the church to help all of God's people realize they are inept and incapable of goodness?

So, let me ask: What if our faith journey is about who we are, rather than who we are not?

Earlier in chapter 4, I mentioned the idea of the early Christian church's holy purpose being a movement that reflected having the mind of Christ and following in "The Way" of this person Jesus. What does this really look like? What does it mean for the 21st Century church? How might this change our behavior in defining whom we accept as the faithful to simply accepting all for who they truly are?

One of the more compelling characteristics of the early Christian movement was how it resonated with those living on the edges of society - the oppressed, the poor, the victimized, the hungry, the widow, the wanderer, the outsider. I don't believe that it resonated with them because it freed them from those circumstances or changed their status. They were still seen through the same societal lens. But I believe it resonated with them because it met them exactly where they were and for whom they were. There were no prerequisites that they had to meet in order to be fully accepted and embraced by this invitation into "The Way". They could be who they were and experience all the benefits of being a loved and cherished child of the living God, without exception.

This 21st Century church desperately needs to examine its behavior and messaging as it relates to this unconditional acceptance and welcome. This flows easily off the tongue but is very difficult to carry out authentically. Yes, there is a passion to love everyone for who they are, but still a propensity to require that people meet certain conditions in order to be loved. Our love is based on who the person is not and who they need to become rather than who they already are. Our love works through a default lens of negativity rather than through the lens of the mind of Christ.

As I have evolved in my own faith and world view, what I see as the most pertinent mission of Jesus' Way is to help each of us be awakened to our true self. I do not believe that we must conform to a rigid rubric of life and behavior in order to be loved. But we have to undo what has clouded our ability to see our true selves. "The Way" and its holy purpose was co-opted by political and military powers, beginning in the 4th Century. The path of "The Way" deviated from its true and beautiful mission of awakening all people to their true purpose and their true self. Instead of the Church embodying the mind of Jesus and loving the faithful for who they were, it created a set of rigid requirements. In order to be loved and be accepted, one had to conform. If you conformed, you were welcome inside the circle of love and faith. If you did not conform, you were outside that circle, and perhaps even killed. This division - this creating of the worthy and the unworthy - cannot and should not embody our vision of our church. And, I am quite confident that this is not what Jesus intended when he commissioned his faithful into living out "The Way".

My dream for this 21st century is that faith communities of all natures and designs embrace this mission to awaken people to their true selves. We must rediscover and reclaim our sense of our holy identity as God's beloved and cherished children. We have the tools and the framework to accomplish this. Genesis says that we are all created in the image of God. This is a powerful statement. It pictures us as not separate or apart from this living God, but connected to the very image and being of this living God. It also asserts that all things were brought into being by God. Nothing exists that is not of God. If that is true, how can we create checklists and boxes that determine who is of God and who is not? All things are of God. Why would we ever want to make our first voice of welcome be "hello, sinner, glad to have a wretch in our midst"? Finally, we claim that there is nothing in all the world that can separate us from this God. Absolutely nothing, no one thing of any imagining, can separate us from this God. It isn't about right belief, right living, or right conformity. It is about the reality that all is of God, and that all of us are connected to and created by this God of love. Once again, it is easy to say this. But we need to live this belief and embrace it as the true revolution of love that Jesus proclaimed love to be.

I do not believe that this dream is a pie-in-the-sky fantasy. I am convinced that there is real hope that faith communities have the capacity to re-imagine their reason for being and advance it with renewed boldness and courage. We can re-envision our holy purpose, our 'why'. It isn't going to be easy, nor should it be. This path of living in and being "The Way" of Christ has no rose garden promises. It is a way that calls us to be in the trenches of life, accept the struggles as sacred, love with no condition, and act with true compassion for the other. That is daunting, but it is also profoundly invigorating.

CHAPTER 7

What If We Replace Quick Fixes with Sacred Struggles?

MY WIFE AND I WERE FORTUNATE TO BE able to take one of our bucket list trips; three weeks traveling through the amazing wine country of Italy. We are what some would call "wine snobs". We prefer "wine connoisseurs". A major part of our trip was spent in the stunningly beautiful region of Tuscany. No words really can do this place justice. Every breathtaking view revealed a valley with vineyards stretching in all directions, and old stone buildings sitting timelessly on the hilltops. At first, we stopped at nearly every turn to capture yet another picture of this indescribable landscape. But, after having done ten or so of these stops, we gave up because there were simply too many stunning vistas to capture.

One day, we were able to meet privately with a winemaker in the Montalcino area of Tuscany. This area proudly produces the famed Brunnello wine. We drove through the hills and valleys of Tuscany, navigating our little car through all the narrow trails. At last we arrived at Cupano, the winery we were visiting that afternoon. Surrounding us was a freshly cultivated field, obviously being prepared to receive new vines.

I was born in the farmlands of South Dakota and have seen newly worked land that revealed rich dark soils for planting. As I looked at the soil in this soon to be vineyard, I couldn't believe how harsh this soil looked. It was hard, gray in tone, and showed no real capacity to nourish anything that would be planted there. I even stopped to take a picture and feel the soil because I was so baffled at its quality. My only thought was, "how can they possible grow anything, let alone grapevines, in this rock-hard stuff?"

Our visit to the Cupano Winery with Lionel, the wine maker, was inspired. He talked with us for nearly two hours, sharing stories of different vintages and explaining his old country method for producing the best wines. He poured us delicious tastings of his most recent releases. We sat outside on the patio of his home admiring the lush countryside and the unique quality of his vintages. Sipping the rich dark red wine reminded me of my earlier questions about the inhospitable-seeming soil. "Do you really plant vines in that harsh looking stuff?" Lionel smiled and stated, "oh Jeff, the Brunello grape needs to struggle. The harsher the soil, the more intense the heat and the less water it receives, the better. The harder this grape has to struggle for life, the more intense the fruit becomes, resulting in the finest of juices. For this grape it is all about the struggle." I was fascinated by his answer. His wonderful, fragrant wine – with its unique taste and character – was the result of effort, not ease. I took inspiration from that, along with a case of his most recent releases.

I tell this story for a reason. Struggle can seem like a four letter word – something to be avoided at all costs. We don't like to struggle. We want quick fixes with instant results and immediate gratification.

It is nearly impossible to avoid this mindset in today's world. We get frustrated if we can't get our pizza delivered to our home in less than an hour. When we place an online order, we expect it to be at our doorstep in no more than a few days. If we have a question, we want the answer within minutes. Getting sick is a nuisance and we want the problem to be taken care of immediately. Having a better diet or exercising is way too difficult. Instead, getting a prescription or having a procedure is easier and faster.

This doesn't just apply to our personal lives. It is very real and present in our churches and the institutions with which they are aligned. Instead of taking a serious look in the mirror to discover how we have contributed to the challenges facing our faith communities today, the easy approach has been to try and invoke every quick fix possible. And, this isn't just a recent trend. In my experience, this practice started way back in the 1970s, which was really the beginning of the great decline for the organized church.

Even though my pastor father hated the idea of abandoning the sacred traditional worship liturgy, he felt he had to try something new to connect with the younger generations. I played a lot of guitar in the 70's and so my dad decided he would put me in front of the church and have me play instrumental guitar music during offering and communion. He had no idea that I was playing covers of the popular bands of the time, Yes, Rush, and Led Zeppelin without the vocals of course. What mattered is worship now included the guitar and that seemed like a surefire solution to attract younger people. Soon, we were bringing camp songs into worship which was then followed by having clowns appear in worship. Literally, there was a movement in the 70's for what was called "clown ministry". Floyd Shaffer was the originator of this idea and did it very well. However, it was co-opted by nearly every youth pastor in the country to try and attract young people. What started as a very meaningful experience quickly turned into a gimmick, and disappeared within a few years.

Sunday School went through similar changes. In the 80's and 90's, a movement spread throughout the country called "rotational Sunday School". It started in a Twin Cities church and gained incredible momentum soon showing up in churches everywhere. Rotational Sunday School integrated drama, music, storytelling, art projects, and much more in an effort to liven up the experience of learning the important lessons from the Bible. Confirmation was not far behind in its efforts to become more relevant. It moved from being taught by the pastor in lecture-form to a more group-centered discussion format. Retreats were incorporated to change up the environment for teaching and learning. Adult mentors were enlisted and service projects were conducted.

The young adults were not going to be left behind either. Over the past few decades, a variety of approaches have attempted to create a more relevant and attractive environment for them. Pub Theology, Beer and Hymns, Women and Wine, Scrap Booking Retreats, Mothers of Preschoolers (MOPS), Emergent Generation Churches and so many more have been tossed out to see what might stick and reverse the trajectory of decline.

One of the companies I lead, Kairos and Associates, is a resource development consulting firm. We focus on helping faith communities develop needed financial resources to allow their mission and ministry to advance in effective ways. A key part of this work is to help nurture cultures of generosity, otherwise known as stewardship ministry. Over the years, it has been frustrating to see how congregations have dealt with the growing challenge of declining financial resources. Our approach is focused on the culture and the individuals that make up that culture. We look at long term efforts to grow the generosity of people for their own sake, not just for the sake of the church. We believe this has a greater chance for long-term and sustainable impact. We also pay attention to a congregation's missional impact - knowing that people want to give to something that is truly making a difference in people's lives and the life of the community.

However, our biggest challenge in implementing our approach is dealing with faith community leaders who want their challenges to be quickly fixed with as little effort as possible. When we meet with leaders to discuss our approach and philosophy, often times, their response is, "but how much money will you raise? How much will our annual giving increase?" In other words, we need the money now. We don't have the time or patience to invest in a long-term strategy to develop a culture of generosity.

There are dozens of quick fix programs that have emerged for churches to use in their stewardship efforts, many of which are simply downloadable programs to help conduct the classic annual stewardship drive for as little effort and cost as possible. Consecration Sundays were the real deal for a number of years because it helped to quickly bring in additional dollars to the budget. Shame, guilt, and obligation were always available strategies when the situation became dire. The problem is that these are simply what they are; quick fixes. They are void of any real ability to nurture and sustain the development of a generous culture.

As financial support has declined, membership has declined as well – especially in worship attendance. Concern has been focused on these basic issues; how do we get people to come back to worship or start coming in the first place? The Church Growth Movement was started in the 80's & 90's. Entertainment evangelism was a catch phrase that emerged out of this movement. Bringing in video technology to the worship experience became a must. Showing videos during sermons, offering live streaming, doing podcasts, and on and on. All done with the hopes that these efforts would quickly fill the pews once again.

All of these efforts have one thing in common. They are all trying to solve problems in quick ways. How do we get more people into our churches? How do we get more money to do the work we believe we need to do? How do we remain relevant and important to people's lives? All of these challenges have been met with good intentions. People truly love their church and want it to survive. But quick fix solutions have not solved our problems. That's because it is the wrong approach - it isn't a question of 'fixing'. The church doesn't need to be 'fixed' in the way we thought. It needs to be completely reimagined and deconstructed so that real meaningful change can happen; change that brings about a transformation of who we are and why we believe we exist in the first place. This is why the phrase "you are just rearranging the chairs on the deck of the Titanic" is so often used these days. Quick fixes have no lasting value, nor do they really get after what needs to be tackled.

When the ELCA was formed over 30 years ago, it merged three different Lutheran bodies. At the time of this merger, these three separate Lutheran bodies brought together over 11,000 congregations. Currently, that same ELCA church has a little over 9,000 congregations and that number is expected to drop significantly in the next few decades. Obviously, whatever quick fixes or solutions the church thought they had have not worked. The church did not accomplish what it intended, and didn't create any lasting outcomes. Our quick-fix approach has radically failed to ask the hard and more difficult questions.

We are in a defining moment. It is a moment that asks us to face our struggle with a deep vulnerability as well as a willingness to think radically in imagining the church's future. Self-examination is crucial. We must acknowledge our own failings and ask ourselves challenging questions. It is essential that we engage in this kind of self-inventory if we are to be a relevant church for today's world.

It isn't easy and it can be painful. It involves what I like to call a sacred struggle. What I loved about our experience with Lionel, the winemaker, is the way he described the journey of the Brunello grape. He didn't express pain or frustration as he talked about the grape's need to experience a difficult struggle in it's journey to becoming fine wine. Instead, he expressed an understanding and a pure satisfaction that the hardship of growing the grape would bring about the vine's greatest potential.

I truly believe that if we can see our future in this way, we will see a beautiful journey of sacred struggle. This struggle will ultimately help us to develop the finest of our possibilities. I am convinced that when we accept struggle as a normal aspect of growth – and legitimize it as a natural part of our faith journey - we will find the resolve to face this moment with courage and boldness. We will embrace our struggle without fear and see struggle as part of our resilience.

I was worshipping at a client's congregation recently and noticed this quote on the front of their worship folder, (formerly known as a bulletin!!). It is a quote from the French Philosopher Pierre Teilhard de Chardin. It said; "Above all, trust in the slow work of God. We are quite naturally impatient in everything to reach the end without delay. We should like to skip the intermediate stages. We are impatient of being on the way to something unknown, something new. And yet it is the law of all progress that it is made by passing through some stages of instability - and that it may take a very long time. And so I think it is with you; your ideas mature gradually - let them grow, let them shape themselves, without undue haste. Don't try to force them on, as though you could be today what time (that is to say, grace and circumstances acting on your own good will) will make of you tomorrow. Only God could say what this new spirit gradually forming within you will be. Give Our Lord the benefit of believing that his hand is leading you. And accept the anxiety of feeling yourself in suspense and incomplete."

This truly is a word of grace for all of us taking on this sacred struggle. It is one that all faith communities, and the leaders of these communities, are experiencing. It is not a trial. It is not a punishment. It is not woe. It is gift, ripe with opportunity and potential. It is the seemingly inhospitable soil in which we must plant our vines – vines, that through struggle, will become hardy and strong. The past can no longer serve us, and what has been is over. Most importantly, it doesn't need to be fixed. What we will become is yet to be discovered and will involve newly imagined ways of being the church. So, we must live in this moment of struggle and let it drive us into courageous action. There are no guarantees or certainty and the outcome is far from determined, but we are stronger and more resilient than we know, because we believe that God is right in the middle of it all.

In my working with congregations facing this time of sacred struggle, I have often shared a video called "Focus Your Vision" by DeWitt Jones. DeWitt Jones is a brilliant photographer who worked for National Geographic and has become a well-known motivational speaker, filmmaker and author. In this video, he talks about being in Alaska trying to shoot some pictures in Glacier Bay and was waiting to be picked up by a bush pilot out in the middle of nowhere to be flown in for the shoot. The pilot never showed up. While becoming more and more furious with this person for being a no-show, a voice in his head said, "look around, Dewitt. Look around at what's wanting to happen right here, right now!" So, he started looking around and suddenly he saw these amazing photo opportunities right there in front of him. Instead of being furious that his original plan hadn't happened, he let go of his frustration. He let go of his plan and engaged with the uncertainty of the moment. He let his creativity take over. He let what was in front of him - right there in that present moment - speak. The photos he was originally sent to capture of Glacier Bay never ended up in the article that was written. Instead, he published only the photos that he allowed himself to discover when his pilot failed to show. The article won him an award.

Being free to face the sacred struggle is as much about letting go as it is about anything else. We need to let go of what we think or want to happen and allow ourselves to see what is right there in front of us. We need to engage with our own uncertainty and let our creative energies percolate. This is incredibly liberating. It frees us from all the baggage we carry into this journey. It pushes us to let go of all the lost hopes we may have had for our church, for our children and for our communities, and allows us to see what is right there in front of us wanting and hoping to happen. This is the real essence of possibility. It is believing that this isn't a moment of woe or collapse or a crisis needing simple fixes. Instead it is a moment of hope and ambition. It is a moment of devotion and desire – for our church and for ourselves. We simply need to see it, embrace it, and allow this moment of sacred struggle to happen without anger, sadness or self-pity. Our sacred struggle should be emboldened with hopefulness and faith in a God that is real and present – here with us.

Letting go of the belief that we require a quick fix, or must simply do better with what we have always done, is essential. We must look at this moment as a time of real transformation. It calls us to look deep within our systems, or practices, or assumptions and begin to deconstruct these and create something completely new and different. We must begin with rediscovering our holy purpose and restoring its clarity. We need to originate a new purpose, and discover the new 'why' God has in store for us. This is a sacred moment that involves struggle, loss and deep challenge. But that isn't a bad thing. It is a beautiful and powerful moment to become something we haven't imagined before. This new identity, this new holy purpose, can be truly life giving. It can awaken us to our true selves - a community that has perhaps lost it's true holy purpose by being and practicing church in ways that have not been helpful or faithful to living in the mind of Christ. Engaging in this difficult work can be our strength and a testament to our resilience. We need to dig deep into ourselves now more than ever. And as the words of Isaiah 41:10 tell us, "do not fear, for I am with you."

CHAPTER 8

What If It's More than Being Service Providers?

M Y LEAST FAVORITE BILLBOARD OF ALL time simply said, "Got Jesus?" It was a take on the milk ads from several years ago that had various people with milk on their mouth and said, "Got Milk?" The billboard gave the reader the impression that you could just walk into a store and 'get yourself some Jesus'. It would be as easy as picking up a gallon of milk.

It's true that the world runs through transaction. We live in a consumerist society. More than that – we live in a capitalist/industrial society that seems to be on consumerist steroids most of the time. Regrettably, the church has often presented itself as a place of transaction, as well. We can come to church and get ourselves some forgiveness, maybe some love, friendship, inspiration, or knowledge. Our consumer minds can manufacture any number of items that we might need to pick up at the church market.

I have visited hundreds of faith communities over my years

of consulting and this mindset is present all too often. Churches have structured themselves as vendors of faith, offering a menu of options to help you acquire that faith. Instead of presenting themselves as a gathering of people invested in a shared journey of missional impact, they are burdened by the pressure to offer a variety of selections and benefits. Churches are expected to provide quality education for all ages, effective ministry groups to serve children, youth, young adults, families, empty nesters and seniors. There are musical groups, worship teams, theater clubs, service outings, etc. Church staffs invest the majority of their time into recruiting volunteers and planning and administering all of these expected services. We blame our members for having a "consumer mentality of church". However, the reality is that the culture itself is designed to perpetuate this expectation.

The hard truth is that this is not sustainable. Churches see dwindling financial and people resources. Despite this, churches continue to obsess over how to mine for new people and new revenue streams – all in the service of keeping these vending machines stocked. This isn't to say that churches need to stop providing meaningful opportunities and experiences for people who are engaging their ministries. However, we need to transform our culture in a substantial way. We cannot be a place of transaction. Instead, we must transform into being a community that is driven and sustained by what we do and why we do it. It can't simply be because 'we are a church.' We need to reach out beyond our own congregations and invest in meaningful partnerships with others. We can no longer be a place in which our mission centers around being providers of services, where people come to get something from us. We need to be a place where people see themselves as integral and vital to living out the mission. It's not a place where something is happening to them, but a place that happens with and through them. It's a partnership, not a vendor relationship.

In the middle of writing this book, I had the amazing opportunity to join one of my clients on a trip to climb Mt. Kilimanjaro in Tanzania, Africa, the highest point on the African continent standing at 19,341 feet. They are a congregation that has a long-standing tradition of hosting backpacking trips for all ages. This time they wanted to go big, so Kilimanjaro it was. I happen to be good friends with the pastor of this church and I couldn't turn down his invitation to join them on this life changing journey.

The method for embarking on a trip of this nature is that you have to hire professional guides to take you to the summit. You can't just park your car at the trailhead and start climbing up the mountain. There are definite dangers and extreme conditions that can be a part of this climb, so having a guide is not only required but critically important. On the surface, it can seem like you are simply making a transaction with your guide company. You pay them a certain amount of money to assist you in making it to the summit. However, after having experienced this climb, this is far from the reality of this relationship.

Planning and prepping for this trip started about 14 months before the actual climb took place. There were meetings with participants and FaceTime conversations with the lead guide from the company hired from Tanzania. Questions were answered, concerns addressed, and directions given. But there was also the encouragement to take this climb seriously and work on preparing yourself both physically and mentally for the journey.

Upon arrival in Tanzania, our guide company hosted us at a farm which served as a base camp. This was to help us get acclimated to life on the mountain. All the tents were set up including the mess tent. Our hiking community was getting established and it was a time of great anticipation as the mountain loomed above us in the background reminding us that this was really about to happen. Our elevation at the farm was about 3,000 feet. Just 15 miles away sat the towering slopes of Kilimanjaro rising to over 19,000 feet. It is hard to describe just how ominous that scene was as we took it in and puzzled over how we were going to climb to the top of that enormous wonder of nature; breathtaking, intimidating, and awe inspiring are about the best I can do in capturing the moment.

At this point we were working on getting to know the people from the company hired to take us to the summit. There were porters to carry gear, cooks to make the meals, assistant guides to lead us on the trail, and people to attend to water needs and other basic tasks at the campsites. It was overwhelming to see just how many people it took to help navigate this adventure. Our group had 22 people, for that it required 73 porters, four cooks and nine assistant guides and one lead guide.

The ultimate goal of everyone who steps on Kilimanjaro is to reach Uhuru Peak, the true summit of the mountain. However, this is not always achievable. The potential for harsh weather, physical fatigue, and the affects of altitude sickness are major contributors to preventing you from accomplishing that ultimate goal. Our company was called Tanzania Choice Safaris. They host dozens of groups every year up the mountain and our lead guide boasted that he had a 100% success rate of getting all of his groups to the summit.

Festo was our fearless and confident lead guide. His years of experience and engaging personality couldn't help but instill confidence and excitement in each of us. From the very moment of our arrival, Festo was working hard to get to know each member of our group. He watched us interact with the other guides and listened to our stories that inspired us to climb Kilimanjaro. It was obvious that this was more than a job for Festo. This was his passion and primary mission in life.

None of us really knew what to expect. We had each done our research and had watched hours of Youtube following others who had made the climb. But none of that can really get you prepared for this experience. There are 40-plus miles of trail and over 15,000 feet of elevation change. In addition, there are five different climate zones on the mountain, starting with a rain forest and ending at the arctic zone. It's cold, windy, and often snowy at 19,000 plus feet. The journey starts with shorts and t-shirts and ends with parkas, goggles, scarves, gators, snow pants and as much smartwool as you can handle.

The route we chose, The Lemosho Trail, is one of the longest to the summit, but offers the highest potential for success. Acclimating to the elevation is essential, so this trail gets you up in elevation and has you stay there for at least five full days. As we hiked together following our guides, the theme words were always "pole, pole," which means "slowly" in Kiswahili. It really isn't a hike, it is a slow snail's pace of a walk. To do otherwise would leave you exhausted and unable to reach the summit. At first, none of us thought we could make it to the summit at the pace we were taking. However, as we got into a rhythm, we started calculating how far each step took us, how long it took to take the step, and what distance we could travel at that pace. Our conclusion was, "Pole, Pole" works.

During the first five days of hiking, it was fascinating to watch our lead guide at work. Festo was constantly encouraging us, asking us questions and assessing how we were doing. Festo would appear at different points along the trail. Sometimes he was on rocks high above us looking down as we walked. Other times he would appear from below, having been watching us from behind. He always showed up with a smile and an encouraging word, asking us how we were feeling and doing. At other points of the climb, Festo would walk alongside each of us individually, engaging us in conversation and getting a feel for how we were handling the conditions. Never did we feel that Festo was evaluating us or telegraphing concern over our ability to make it to the summit. It was as natural and authentic as could be.

After six days on trail, we arrived at the base camp known as the Barafu camp. It is the final destination for all the various trails. All trails lead to Barafu and from there you climb to the summit. The camp sits at about 15,000 feet. From Barafu you climb another 4,000 feet up over a three mile stretch. The summit experience starts at night anywhere between midnight and 2:00AM. The purpose is to get you to the summit when the sun rises and the clouds have not yet engulfed the mountain. We arrived at the base camp late in the afternoon and were given about six hours of time to rest and prepare for the climb. To think that you would actually get some sleep was crazy. All we could think about was the enormity of this final part of our journey. During the evening, as we were resting in our tents, a wind came up the likes of which we had not yet experienced. Our first six days of climbing had been without any real weather challenges; Sunshine, low winds, no rain, and very reasonable temperatures. That was all about to change. While lying in my tent, I could feel the wind getting stronger and stronger, slamming the sides of my tent and ripping at the flaps. It was so strong I had to keep reminding myself that these tents were designed to survive in this very situation.

The winds became ferocious. Given the conditions, I felt there was no way we were going to be allowed to climb to the summit. It seemed way too dangerous to put us on that ridge in the dark climbing up the steep trail. I was wrong. At 1:00AM, a voice outside my tent yelled, "it's time to summit." I couldn't believe it as the wind hadn't died down. Instead, it had gotten stronger. But we were actually going to attempt this. I exited my tent and began to assemble my gear for the climb. I pulled on layer upon layer in hopes of staying warm and protected from the intense wind. The gusts had to have been over 60 mph. It was frightening, but we strapped on our headlamps and zipped up our parkas. At first, I thought there was snow falling, but no, it was dust particles being blown hard through the air, and hitting us in the face. Not only did we have to worry about the altitude, we now had to be concerned for our eyes being blinded by the dust. And, it felt like the wind could blow us off the mountain itself. I was once again humbled by how nothing could fully prepare me for this.

Once assembled, Festo gave us instructions for how we would take on the summit. He wanted us to try our best to stay in one group, stopping very infrequently, and keeping a very steady pace. His concern was keeping us warm in these conditions. Stopping would only prevent that. We began together "pole, pole". As we hiked out of camp, we passed other tent compounds that were being decimated by the wind. Tent poles were breaking and debris was being strewn everywhere. Again, the thought of actually doing this in these conditions seemed insane. Yet, we pressed on.

The first half of the summiting adventure was brutal. It took everything we had just to fight the wind and keep our balance, especially in the dark with just headlamps to guide our path. At one point, one of our group members, who was 65 years and weighed maybe 100 pounds, was nearly blown off the trail. But for the skill of one of our guides, she would have been seriously injured. As she was feeling herself being lifted off the ground, she suddenly felt a hand grab her from behind and bring her back to her feet. The guide had been strategically placed behind her to assist as needed. That was true for the rest of us, as well, knowing in total we had nine guides plus our lead guide, Festo, who were assigned to hike with us to the summit.

About three quarters of the way up to the volcano plateau called "Stella's Point," I was at a breaking point. I was trying my best to keep the steady pace that the guides had set, but my body was so fatigued by the wind I was losing strength. Finally, I said to myself, "I can't do this. I need to stop." Just as I was feeling this, I sensed another guide right behind me. His name was Erasto. We had become acquainted during the first several days of the trip. He was positioned right behind me. As I was processing the possibility that I wasn't going to make it to the summit, Erasto appeared and said, "let me take your poles and your pack. You can do this." I responded saying, "this is so hard, I don't know if I can." He looked at me with this gentle smile and said, "It is hard for me too. We can do this together."

I gave him my poles but kept my pack. I was too proud to give him all my gear. We turned towards the summit and began a different strategy, one that would align with where my body was or wasn't. I was able to put one foot in front of the other, stopping on numerous occasions just to recoup some strength and take in deep and long breaths. I wasn't experiencing any altitude sickness, just extreme fatigue. "Pole Pole", small step by small step, we made our way up the mountain.

At Stella's Point we caught up to the rest of the group. This volcanic plateau is known as the false summit of Kilimanjaro. You feel as though you have reached the top, but you haven't. From this location you must climb *another* 400 plus feet up to Uhuru Peak. At this point we discovered that half of our group was still far down the trail, five of whom were experiencing altitude blindness. What, you can go blind as well? Thank goodness we were not aware that this was even a possibility. In addition, one of our Tanzanian guides started experiencing something called "optic swelling" and couldn't see either. He too needed help. Suddenly, the roles were getting switched up. Not only did we need to be led, we also now needed to lead.

In the end, every single member of our group made it to Stella's Point. All but one of us made it to Uhuru Peak (Festo still claims 100% success rate). In total, the summit day climb took over 16 intense hours involving 4,000 feet of steep elevation and nearly 10,000 feet of descent.

What I realized as we trekked down the mountain to our last campsite; we had not hired a vendor to guide us up to the summit of Kilimanjaro. Instead, we had entered into a significant and symbiotic partnership. Both parties were intimately connected and dependent upon the other. For six full days, Festo had watched and observed, learned and discovered who we were, both physically and mentally. As he gathered this intimate knowledge of us, he was preparing to strategize with the other assistant guides as to how to help us navigate on summit day. With precision, Festo had placed each guide in specific locations amongst our group, knowing what potential needs might arise. And sure enough, each and every member of our group experienced something on that summit day that required our guides to step in and help make it happen. They were as invested and committed to this adventure as we were. They had as much at stake as we did. Without them, it never would have been possible. We knew we were dependant upon them, but we learned that they were also dependant upon us. Having one of their guides experience temporary blindness was a game changer, and our group stepped in to serve his needs as he had served ours.

This was no transactional relationship with a vendor of services. It became a deeply shared mission, a journey that we never could have imagined, and one that would have never been completed without everyone seeing themselves as integral to the journey's unfolding. To have it happen in any other way would have made it impossible to accomplish the mission. We had to do it together, not as separate entities. No one piece was more important than any other. No one simply gave and no one simply took. Every single participant played a critical role in empowering the entire group to reach the summit. When we had doubts, we were encouraged. When we were overconfident, we were humbled. But we committed to the journey regardless of our immediate success. After all, it can take more than one trip up the mountain to summit. But regardless of success, failure, or a qualified combination of the two, it was incredible to have been a part of such a life changing experience.

When I first agreed to join my client in the adventure to climb Kilimanjaro, much of what motivated me was selfish. It would help me get into better shape. I would have an experience that few have ever had. It would allow me to get back to Africa. But, looking back on what transpired, this experience became far more than having reached Uhuru Peak. This was a time of deep self-discovery. More importantly, it was a time that exposed me in new ways to the power that comes when we allow ourselves to be dependent upon others to accomplish a mission.

This experience has now become a working metaphor for how I see the challenges facing our church. It is a time that is far too difficult and mysterious to go it alone. We cannot afford to continue living as separate entities, those who provide and those who receive. In and of itself, this is not a terrible thing - to give in order that others may receive. It simply is not sustainable, nor fully reflective of our missional identity.

Somehow we need to get back to a culture that experiences itself completely intertwined as one body, all working together to achieve a goal. As Paul says in 1 Corinthians 12:20, "there are many members, yet one body." Every single person is integral to the success of the whole. Living faithfully in "The Way", having the "mind of Christ", draws us into a healthy co-dependency. The ebb and flow of giving and taking is shared equally. Sometimes I need to receive. Sometimes I need to give. Sometimes, I need to do both simultaneously.

A common lament I hear amongst church leaders is, "our volunteers are burning out and it's the same people always doing the work." Perhaps a deeper examination of why this is happening may break the mold. When the church continues to project the impression that you can come get something, great Sunday school, awesome music, dynamic adult studies, etc., it will remain vulnerable to burnout. It doesn't create a sense of shared mission or shared holy purpose. The constant pressure to fill the vending machine with services, and keep finding the bodies necessary to make sure the machine is running, is exhausting.

A key starting point in helping to make this shift away from vendor to shared partnership is to simply look at how you message yourself in both word and action. What are the impressions you create that influence people's expectations for what they will experience when they are in your midst? Do you message and model in ways that communicate that you are a place where you will get something? Or, do you message and model in ways that let people understand that this is a place to invest yourself in living out "The Way" of being that is relational and interdependent upon all those engaged?

The safari company we hired to guide us up Kilimanjaro had this as a part of their mission and values: "By the time you board your plane to Tanzania, we want you to feel not as though you have hired us for your safari, but as though you are coming here to visit us as your friends." This is not an impression that makes you feel that you are simply going to come and get served. Part of their job was to create an environment in which all of us would *try*. And try together. The message was "we are in this together, like family." We would struggle together, face the hardships together, and have a shared goal. It was a culture of inclusion that didn't minimize the efforts required. We knew it was going to be hard work and we would face it together.

We do play a significant part in creating the culture that perpetuates the idea that we are to provide services for you to consume. As I mentioned, this isn't all bad. We want to be a mission that gives itself away for the sake of others. However, if the experience people are having while engaged in our mission is that it is something being done for them rather than with them, it will be very difficult to move the needle. How we speak, act and expect matters. Changing that dynamic takes discipline, intentionality and a willingness to make substantive changes that are systemic in nature, not just cosmetic. We need to acknowledge the hardships that we are facing and remember that we may not make it to the summit the first time.

So, is it possible to function as a place of service provision and be effective and grow your reach and impact? Yes. But the question still remains, is that how we want to imagine the future of our church? Do we want to be wed to that kind of static service-providing vision?

CHAPTER 9

What if Tomorrow Looks Nothing Like Yesterday?

THE SAGRADA FAMILIA IS AN ARCHITEC-
tural wonder in Barcelona, Spain. It is considered architect
Antoni Gaudi's most brilliant work. The church was started in 1882
and is still under construction today. Gaudi himself worked on this
masterpiece for over 40 years, yet was only able to finish just one
portion of the Nativity facade during his lifetime. This Nativity scene
is but one of the building's three main facades. Gaudi was not the
first architect hired to build this Basilica honoring the Holy Family
of Jesus. The original architect resigned a year into construction when
Gaudi took over as chief architect. He soon transformed this Roman
Catholic church through his unique talent-from its original and fairly
traditional neo-Gothic revival style into a Gaudi masterpiece.

Despite Gaudi not living to see the continued construction of
this inspired work, it was his vision that shaped and informed every
design stage along the way. He left detailed notes about his dream

structure, along with models that he created for each phase of the building. In his final years, he worked tirelessly in both building the project and laying out his vision for its completion. Given the magnitude of the work, he was very aware that he would never live to see it through completion. Today, all three of the facades have been constructed, two being fully complete. The hope is that the final stones will be laid by 2026 to celebrate the fulfillment of this vision on the 100th anniversary of Gaudi's death at the age of 73.

In more ways than one, the Sagrada Familia is a testament of how an inspired vision can be carried on far longer than those who have imagined it. The Segrada Familia Basilica wasn't just a testament to Gaudi's personal vision, it was a vision intended to be experienced by the religious faithful long after the hands that designed and built it were gone. Gaudi was not designing a church just for his own lifetime, but a sacred space whose existence would stretch far into futures yet unimagined. I want to add that if seeing this church is not yet on your bucket list, I urge you to make it one of your top ten. There truly is nothing like in the world.

Just as Gaudi envisioned his building being relevant for future generations, so we, too, must imagine our church being relevant to those who have yet to experience it. Although we may hope that our new vision of our future is one that we can accomplish immediately, this just isn't realistic. But despite our current despair over the decline of our church, we need to recognize that we are in it for the long haul. I recently heard Reggie McNeal speak at a Church Leadership Conference. Reggie is a well-known church leader, author and speaker around the country. He was addressing the difficult subject of the decline in our church and what it might look like in the not so distant future. He said something that really resonated with me. In essence he said, "the church we have known and experienced will most likely go away. The institutions, the denominational bodies, the practices we have become so familiar with will probably dissolve. But what is also true is that something new will emerge that is more capable and relative to what the church needs to be for the future. It may not happen for another 50 years, but it will happen."

One of the hardest things for church leaders to accept is that what has been will never be again. This is a very tough nut to swallow. But there is a corollary to this; what is to come is not here yet. Living in these in-between times is extremely difficult, but it is within these two moments that hope and vision can live. And working through this in-between moment is of the utmost importance. The challenge is to not let our own personal wants and needs become paramount to what is at hand. If we are being called to imagine an entirely new way of being the church- of gathering as people of faith, people of the way - we must accept that this full transformation may not happen in our lifetime. But that cannot be a barrier to calling us to act and move this moment forward.

My great-grandfather was a first generation Swedish immigrant to this country. He came as a young man in his twenties and settled down in the Twin Cities of Minnesota. He was very fortunate to find a good job and was able to carve out a fairly comfortable life for him and his family. One of his dreams was to build a small lake cottage in northern Minnesota, something that would remind him of the old country. That dream was realized later in his life when he purchased 400 feet of lakeshore on Two Inlets Lake, just a few miles south of Itasca State Park, the home of the Mississippi Headwaters (he paid $5/foot for lakefront!).

As you drove into this beautiful piece of property, you were greeted by hundreds of towering clump birch trees, the kind that had 10-12 trunks on each tree. It was a spectacular location for his small cottage – a cottage that included a classic stone fireplace made from stones he gathered himself from that very piece of land.

Soon after he completed his cottage, he began the work of planting over 1,000 balsam fir trees. People would ask him why he was doing this when there were these incredibly beautiful birch trees already surrounding his cottage. He never answered, just kept planting the trees. Today, as you enter this beautiful piece of property, you are greeted by hundreds of towering balsam firs. The birch trees have all disappeared, felled by age, weather and time.

My great-grandfather's dream was not just for himself – it was for the future of this plot of land. He knew that those birch trees were coming to the end of their journey as they live to be about 60-70 years old. It was time for something new to emerge, and he decided it was time for the balsam fir. He was nearly 80 years old when he began planting his 1,000 plus trees. He knew he would never see those trees mature in his lifetime. He would never even see them begin to grow, but he knew they would. He trusted in the land and his work. It wasn't about him, it was about his family, and their families. It was about me, his great-grandson and my children, and their children. And now, decades later, those very balsam fir trees are coming to the end of their journey. It is time to imagine, again, what comes next. It is our turn to invest in what is yet to become.

What tree is waiting to emerge that will take the shape of the church in this in-between time? It will be something that will be the framework for a church that is yet to be realized. Our actions can't be focused on just satisfying ourselves and our own solace. We need to be laying the groundwork for future generations of the faithful. We need to see how the world is changing and imagine how it will continue to change. Our ability to see forward for the sake of the future is vitally important. Without that, we can't be the kind of change agents necessary for the church. We won't be able to help it transform into something new and beautiful.

A few years ago I was hired by a congregation with the intention of helping them address the challenge of having a very worn-out facility that no longer served their ministry needs. They needed help in discerning what their options were, as well as identifying the kind of resources that might be available to help them take on this challenge. As we do with every client, I began with a deep listening process. The purpose is twofold; to give leaders the necessary input and information to make good decisions, and to allow the people of the faith community to have their voices heard. Both are essential in bringing about the best possible outcomes.

As I engaged the listening process, two things became very clear. First, this congregation lacked any real sense of their purpose at this point in time. It was a congregation that had experienced incredible growth back in the 50's, 60's and 70's and now was struggling to pay the bills. Secondly, the members had little to no energy to consider giving any financial resources, being all too aware that there was no real direction or vision for the future.

When I was hired by this congregation, the leadership team had informed me that they had done some preliminary work in assessing their facility needs. Their conclusion was that they needed to tear down the entire education and office wings and start from scratch. Their estimate for the project was about $13 million. For nearly every mainline congregation in the country, that is an overwhelming objective.

When I finished with my listening process, I gathered the leadership together to share my report. I knew this was going to be hard for them to hear as I was about to tell them that moving forward with a $13 million project was not in the cards. What I did share is that if they agreed to invest in a deeper visioning process that allowed them to capture a better sense of their purpose and plan for their ministry's future, that would translate into greater energy amongst their membership. However, I qualified that by saying that even with this effort, the likelihood of raising $13 million wasn't remotely possible. I encouraged them to wait to look at their facility needs until after they had conducted the visioning process. Once that was completed, I advised them to consider a more modest goal of six - eight million dollars, which still would be a stretch.

Over the next three months I walked the leadership through a series of actions and discussions trying to help them discover and articulate what they believed their holy purpose was for this moment in time. Why were they being called to do the things they were planning to do, and how were they going to make it happen? It was difficult for them because many of the leaders around the table had been at this church for decades. They couldn't get themselves wrapped around the idea that something new needed to emerge. They were fixated on doing something that would bring back the good old days - because that is who they were and needed to be once again.

All throughout this process there were three or four leaders who kept pushing back at every step. They kept saying, "why do we have to do this? Why can't we just go ahead with our $13 million plan? We know we can do this! We are (put your favorite church name here) after all!" As much as I wanted to embrace their enthusiasm, I had to keep reminding them that those days were never coming back. It was time for a new vision for this ministry's future. This didn't have to be seen as a negative in anyway. It could be a great moment of opportunity to live and evolve into something new and impactful.

As I was planning my next trip to work with this church, I received a call from the pastor. I could tell immediately that something was wrong, so I waited to hear the story. He proceeded to tell me in a fairly uncomfortable way that they had come to a place where they needed to discontinue our relationship. It was clear that the three or four leaders who were constantly pushing back were unwilling to engage with the process I was implementing. They were adamant that the church needed to advance with their $13 million plan regardless of what their consultant was telling them. And not just their consultant, but the vast majority of their congregation. Sometimes it's not easy being the messenger.

The heartbreak for me in this whole process was that the opportunity for this ministry to do the hard work of imagining a new future was hijacked by a small group of leaders who couldn't let go of what they believed the church needed to be. For them, it wasn't about the new possibilities and opportunities that awaited their ministry. It was about reclaiming their status from the past. It was about harkening back to something that was never going to return. They were a major player in the community 30 years ago and they were determined to be a major player yet again. This $13 million building project was the only option they saw for making that happen. Their need for this was greater than whatever the needs of the greater faith community might be.

At the same time as I was hitting a wall with these church leaders, I had another client in a very similar situation. They had a tired and worn out facility that had lost its capacity to adequately serve it's ministry. In addition, it was a very historic building with beautiful stained glass windows that needed serious attention. When I was brought on board, the leadership had determined they needed to raise money to save those windows because this church was such an important landmark in their community.

Again, I began the work by doing some deep listening. What

I discovered wasn't all that different from the other client. There was little sense of purpose or clear direction for the church's future. Additionally, there was little to no energy to give resources to a building project. One of the most important messages I heard from the members was, "we don't want the stained glass windows to become our mission."

When I met with the leadership to share my report, it was received in a much different way. When I said they needed to take the time to discover a new sense for their holy purpose and rethink how they should address their building needs, they all breathed a sigh of relief. Deep down, they all knew that doing a project just to save their windows was a non-starter. It was important, but not missionally driven. They just needed to restart their imaginations so that they could think differently about their future.

I recommended they put together a dream team that would be tasked with doing some broad listening to the people in their local community. The intent was to get a better sense of what those community needs actually were. Then, when this process was completed, they were tasked with doing an analysis of their building to discover how it could be reimagined to meet some of those newly discovered needs. Instead of pushing back on this recommendation, they took it on with inspired energy and enthusiasm. They had been struggling with what to do about their church and a ministry that seemed to be stuck. Now, they were given an opportunity to believe that there was more to their story than a tired old building. Something new was waiting to be discovered. They could find renewal and direction with a newly framed holy purpose.

These were two very similar situations with two very different outcomes. One was clinging to the glory days of the past and could see no other way forward. The other felt a sense of freedom in letting go of their original dream and embracing something completely new and different - something that was yet unknown but inspired tremendous energy and excitement.

It is not an overstatement to say that we are at a critical time that calls us to take a step back and look seriously at who we are and why we exist. As I mentioned in chapter four, taking a new look at our 'why' - that deeper sense of holy purpose for mission - is of utmost importance. And, in doing so there are some crucial things we must remember, and accept.

1. This isn't easy. It is a sacred struggle rather than a quick fix proposition. There is no manual for how to move forward, just the belief that God is still alive and present. We need to trust that God is calling us to move forward with hope and courage.

2. We can't go back to the future. Our past is the past and it can't be reclaimed. There is something new wanting to happen. If we can't let go of the past, then all our efforts will be for naught. We can't imagine something new by hoping it looks like something long gone.

3. This process requires collaboration. It isn't a top down or isolated movement deliberated over by a small group of leaders and disseminated to the masses. For this to truly bear fruit, it must be done with all voices being heard, and not just the voices sitting in our pews. Listening to our neighbors and hearing voices of diversity, in both culture and faith expression, is vital in helping us discover how the church can look into the future. We are not the sole keepers of truth and practice. There are many ways to encounter the holy. Learning from that and appreciating its message will

go a long way in moving us into a new way of being faith communities together.

4. Finally, this is a process that will take time. Like Gaudi's Basileca and my great-grandfather's fir trees, we may not see its full fruition. It is a change that will evolve over many years. This in-between time requires perseverance and dedication. We must do this work, not just for our own sake but for the sake of many generations to come. The only way to bring this about is to start acting differently now and trust that something amazing will unfold as it evolves. We need to do this with courage and with faith.

CHAPTER 10

What If We Have the Ability to Move Forward?

I DON'T WANT TO PRESCRIBE WHAT CHURCH should be. Every culture and every situation will call for something different and unique. Each will need to embrace their own heritage and examine what led to this particular moment. The community and leadership will need to make decisions within their own specific capacities and context. What I would like to provide are some best practices, or mindsets, that I believe are helpful in moving forward into this time of awakening and discovery. There are many ways to imagine this work and advance its efforts. These are simply the things I have come to appreciate over the decades of time I have spent in the trenches of church culture and consulting with leaders around the country.

Creating a Culture of Psychological Safety

In nearly every church culture I have encountered there exists some element of discomfort or dysfunction in it's ability to address various issues, from the difficult to the mundane. These issues can be as serious as pastoral leadership concerns to as simple as using salt verses sand to prevent icy sidewalks. Regardless of the sensitivity and vulnerability of the issue, it is important that the culture allows for healthy and productive dialogue to occur. Otherwise, there is little chance of progress being made, no matter the topic of conversation.

What I have laid out are questions that I believe carry some very sensitive and deeply personal issues. Some will be easier to discuss than others. For a faith community to have the ability to navigate these conversations in productive and healthy ways, there needs to be a culture of psychological safety. This kind of culture doesn't just happen – it requires serious intentionality in order to create that kind of culture. It is a concept that I have just recently come to embrace. As our consulting teams have encountered more and more conflicted church contexts, we see how paralyzed they can be in their ability to have healthy and safe conversations. We have had to work more intentionally at instilling practices within these cultures that create psychological safety for those engaged in the community.

Simply stated, this effort involves setting rules and norms within the culture that allow participants to feel safe on a variety of levels. Every person brings their own back story and DNA into the community. If there are no standards - or rules for engagement - conversations and interactions can quickly spiral out of control, thus nothing productive is accomplished. The primary focus of establishing psychological safety is making sure that people feel safe in being able to share their views. Each person needs to feel secure in expressing their own identity and perspective without fearing that there will be negative reactions and consequences.

Early in my career, I understood this practice as consensus building. But consensus building often falls short of truly honoring a person's feelings and perspectives by making them acquiesce to the action needing consensus. Creating a culture of psychological safety isn't about getting to a consensus. It is all about getting to a place of comfort in having the conversation in the first place. In order for the difficult questions to be discussed productively, this effort needs to be done with real authenticity and integrity.

There are a number of great resources out there to help guide this process. The Joshua Group (www.the-joshuagroup.com), one of the organizations I lead is a primary resource in addressing this process. We have learned a great deal in how to help congregations make significant progress in creating these cultures. In addition, one of our trusted partners in this work is Turning West Consulting (www.turningwest.com), which has designed a very focused process to equip cultures in this important effort. There are other easily accessed online resources that can help guide and equip communities in setting the table for this effort. These resources will help move your faith community into healthy and productive conversations. Don't underestimate how critical healthy and safe conversations are.

Owning the Time of Loss and the Need to Let Go

So much of the emotion around these issues comes out of a feeling of loss rather than just a fear of change. The more we can accept our losses, the more likely it is that we will be able to move in new directions. Nonetheless, the loss of what we have come to love about our church and what it has meant to our lives is not easy to accept. For many, it is all they have known. To think that this version of church is disappearing can be unbearable to imagine. To simply say, "change is inevitable, so deal with it" is quite unhelpful, if not hurtful. The existence of change is not new, but our experience of loss is.

Anyone who has gone through difficult loss knows the challenges that accompany that loss. Sometimes, we cope by trying to pretend that the loss hasn't happened. It's a losing proposition, and usually leads to feeling stuck – which in turn leads to more despair. But if we can allow the pain of loss to be felt and identified – if we look it in the face - we have a better chance of moving through it and past it. For some, this may not be possible. For others, it is possible - as long as there is compassion and empathy for these feelings and a recognition that they are both legitimate and real.

Several years ago, I had the opportunity to work with a legendary congregation. Throughout their years of ministry, they had been led by pastors who later became very prominent leaders within their national church body. Some became bishops, others became successful authors and national speakers. Some moved on to develop successful entrepreneurial endeavors within the church culture. Interestingly, nothing significant in terms of church growth and impact was happening while these leaders served. Only after these leaders had left serving this church did they achieve some level of recognition. However, when you entered this church, you were immediately greeted by the wall of fame. There, all along the hallway, were the pictures of all these pastors who had gone on to become well known leaders. None of their fame was due to their work with this congregation, but the church had yoked itself to this image of who they were; a storied church with legendary leaders. It was a daunting visual for any new pastor beginning their tenure there. They were immediately working in the shadow of 'legends'.

This church hired me to be their consultant. Once I had established a level of trust with their leadership, I recommended that they take down this wall of fame. It only served as a reminder of what this church had believed it was - a kind of incubator for pastors who became great leaders after they left. It was a huge barrier that constantly got in their way of moving their ministry into new and different places. Even if these leaders had created the kind of impact people believed they had, it still worked against them. It blocked their ability to see themselves in the present. They would only be able to move into a new future of hope and possibility when they let go of this past.

Finally, after two years, they took the wall of fame down and moved it into a room in their lower level. They still were hanging onto their wall, but it was no longer the first thing you experienced when entering the church. There was, of course, some serious blowback, but the leaders stuck to their decision. They didn't put the wall of fame back, but it still took another five years for this church community to fully let go of what that wall represented to them. They needed time to accept that those days were gone and were never to return. Even more importantly, they needed to realize that their sense of glory was never real in the first place. It was a loss to many, but in confronting the hold it had over them, they were able to imagine a different future without it. Now, they are imaging what they can become, rather than living in and through the past. But this never would have happened if they hadn't been able to really let go.

Several years ago, a congregation in the Midwest faced the difficult decision that they needed to close their doors. They were a rural congregation and their attendance had dwindled to around 10-12 worshippers a Sunday. Obviously, that was an unsustainable situation. However, instead of just shutting their doors and calling it a day, they brought in some outside council to help them work through the grief of this decision. Through their grief counseling process, the church members were encouraged to see that loss doesn't have to be experienced as a kind of death. It can also be an opportunity for something new to emerge. They were challenged with the idea of how they could turn this moment into an opportunity.

As they were making their plans, they discovered that a bible camp in their synod needed a new chapel. One of the remaining members of the congregation had heard about this, and brought it to the members. "What if we give our church away to this camp?" The camp was 100 miles away – something not lost on the members. But before the meeting was over, they unanimously agreed that not only would they donate their church building to this camp, they would use the remaining $70,000 in their bank account to pay for the move of their building. This story was so moving that it became a news feature on a major Midwest television station. Now, this building that had touched so many lives through its history of ministry would have new life. It would continue a new legacy of faith. Out of the depths of loss, something new and life-giving emerged. They had grieved the loss of their church's original mission and life, but could rejoice in finding it's new purpose. It didn't magically erase their sense of loss, but in accepting it, they found a way to let it go.

We need to own this time of loss so we can grieve appropriately and be better positioned to create a new story for our future.

No Apologies Necessary

In the 90's, the push in churches was to abandon their institutional identity. This was done in hopes of becoming more attractive to the unchurched or non-churched. But one of the tragic consequences was that churches seemed to be apologizing for their identity. Because there was no missional clarity around these actions - other than to try and look different to outsiders – they abandoned things that actually mattered to their identity and authenticity.

Besides dropping the denominational identity from a church's name (Christ Lutheran becoming Christ Church), one of the best examples of this was in the jettisoning of liturgical worship. Many churches decided that this was a turnoff to the younger generations. They changed the style of worship and "modernized" its practice, thinking it would be the perfect solution. Enter "Praise Worship"; Five opening songs with at least five repeats in each, a prayer, scripture reading, sermon, another prayer that basically repeated the sermon you just heard, maybe an offering, closing song and out. Lost in this shift was the rich liturgical history that helped tell the story of faith and practice for many of these churches. It was a kind of self-inflicted wound that didn't accomplish its objective while doing damage in the process.

We shouldn't apologize for who we are. We shouldn't apologize for what has led us to this place and why we practice and believe the way we do. We just need to be authentic with our practice so that others can discover the value and experience the impact on their lives and the lives of others.

I read a story about a missionary who was trying to work with the Native American population of the Plains to convert them to Christianity. At one point, this missionary asked one of the tribal leaders why they slept on the ground. He asked, "why they didn't use cots or bunk beds to keep them off the ground?" The tribal leader responded by saying, "we don't understand why you want to sleep on beds separating you from the ground. For us, the ground is our mother, it is the very source of our life, and we want to be as close to

Mother Earth as possible." For this Native American culture, it was a serious spiritual practice to sleep on the ground and be as close to their source of life as possible. This leader wasn't going to apologize for their practice because it didn't make sense to this missionary. Instead, he proudly proclaimed it as a vital reflection of who they are and what they believe.

There is much about our faith and practice that has life-giving power. We should not feel compelled to abandon those things or throw them out in order to be more attractive to today's generations. We have not lost our core values of following "The Way" of Christ. Those are still very real and very relevant.

When we tell others that if they don't agree or adhere to our practices and beliefs that they will be thrown into the fire, that is when we cross a crucial line. It is not true, nor is it necessary for us to cross this line. We don't have to declare this, or condemn those who don't agree with us, in order to be faithful to our true core values. There are a myriad of belief systems to be experienced, appreciated, and followed. We are not the only game in town, so to speak. However, we are one of the players and we have the ability to extend a powerful invitation to live a life of meaning and holy purpose. And for that, we need not apologize.

Seeing the Quick Fix for What it is

When we experience loss, or the feeling of becoming irrelevant, the normal reaction is to want that feeling to go away as quickly as possible. It is uncomfortable and often times debilitating to live with these feelings. We want to fix it as soon as we can. As hopeful as that instinct may feel, there is no short term quick fix that has long term impact. We need to separate our desire for that quick remedy from what is actually needed. Instead, let us take a deep breath, and look at a long-term investment in change so that our decisions and actions will have meaning and lasting impact.

This is such a central struggle for the consulting organizations I lead. Our methodology is designed to go deep into the cultures we are working with and examine them. We take time to learn and discover what and who they are. Only then do we have the necessary knowledge to help them make critical decisions for the future. It can be a frustrating process. Leaders who are anxious for quick remedies struggle to see the value of taking the time to listening, learn and discover what is being called for in their situation. However, taking the time to gather good input, and being intentional about the discernment process always leads to better decisions. Too often we see leaders looking for the quick, one-time downloadable fix they think will solve their problems, and in as little time as possible. But making major systemic and culture shifts doesn't come quickly, easily, or through any downloadable process.

We live in a world of instant gratification and expedited solutions. Investing in a long-term strategy to bring about meaningful change seems archaic and (in the current vernacular) 'old-timey'. But this approach is how we must work to imagine a new way of being the church. It will not happen overnight, nor should it. It has taken us 500 years to live into our current way of being church. We can't possibly hope that in this moment, which calls for radical rethinking, that any meaningful shifts can happen in a matter of months or years. Instead, this is a journey of decades and perhaps centuries. As good as this would feel to have all figured out within a few years just isn't possible. There is a reason for the term "patience is a virtue". We have found virtue in lasting these past 500 years. We need to find virtue in living out a new future for the next 500.

Being Authentic

One of the biggest consequences of the church growth movement - and many of the subsequent movements that followed - were the disingenuous actions that it created. Many of the decisions were not driven by a clear sense of purpose or missional identity. They were driven by the desire to become more attractive to a constituency that was disappearing. We told ourselves that if we just become this, or do that, more people will come. It was of utmost importance to do whatever was necessary to bring young people and families back into our churches.

To be clear, it isn't a bad thing to want to see more people engage a ministry that you feel strongly about. We want to bring value and impact to people's lives. But when we don't clearly reflect who we are, we fail. We can't twist ourselves into unrecognizability in the hopes of adding more congregation members and more contributor dollars.

The challenge is having a clear sense of your holy purpose, or missional identity. As was discussed in previous chapters, this is critical. Without that clarity, churches will not be equipped to navigate these interesting and opportune times. You can't be authentic to something you don't understand. So, naming it, claiming it, and living into your unique holy purpose is essential to being authentic with your actions.

A current client embodies the importance of this. They are located on the outer edges of a very large metropolitan community. They have invested in being a multi-site mission, not for the purposes of trying to attract more people, but to live more fully into what they see as their missional identity. They did the hard work of digging deep into their DNA to discover what they believed identified them as a faith community. They worked to best articulate their sense of holy purpose. Their ministry was making a difference, and growing on many levels, but they didn't quite have the language to define the fundamental "why" behind what they were doing. But they ultimately had their eureka moment. When they asked themselves why they were engaged in their ministry's work, the answer that emerged was, 'because people matter'. That was it. It sounded uncomplicated but acting on the principle that people mattered took energy, creativity, as well as faith and commitment. Everything they did was truly driven by the fact that all people mattered. They engaged in ministries at multiple sites in an effort to expand their impact on people's lives, not to attract more members.

They lived out this mission at one of their sites which was a very low-income and underserved community, about ten miles from their main campus. This community had experienced a significant population decline during a time of job losses and housing market crashes. The city leaders had decided to try and ignite new growth by offering the community empty lots for $50 each. For this congregation, it was a golden opportunity to create a presence there and care for a people that they felt mattered. So, they bought two vacant lots but not to build a building or start a worshiping community, but to plant an apple orchard and a community garden with a picnic area instead.

Shortly after the apple trees were planted, it was discovered that all of the trees had been stolen. Instead of throwing up their hands in frustration, they just planted another hundred apple trees on the same lot. They were not going to be intimidated out of that community. They were committed to be true to their sense of mission. People mattered. Those people mattered and deserved to know that they were cared about by others.

Now, several years into this commitment, there is a deep relationship with the neighbors within that community. This church is not seen as an invasive intruder haranguing the people who live there, but as a thoughtful partner who is genuinely present because they care about the community. The neighbors join in on the apple harvest and protect the orchard. They have taken ownership of that orchard and their connection to this ministry. They tend the garden, gather for picnics, and invest in deepening their relationship with this faith community. No bible studies are held and no building is being built. Through this orchard and garden, the congregation has invested in simply being present and caring for this community. Lives are being changed because this congregation is being authentic to who they are and genuinely living out its mission. Authenticity matters! More importantly, claiming and living into your holy purpose allows this to happen.

Resilient Leadership

Advancing plans and ushering forward needed change isn't easy. It can often come with a price, or significant conflict. However, these moments of resistance cannot be the deterrent from moving forward. Instead, there needs to be leadership, both lay and clergy, with the resolve and resilience to stay the course. Otherwise we will simply default into old patterns of being church and never discover what this new church can become. Conflict averse cultures won't grow or move into the future. Where there is a passionate and invested leadership system that believes in taking risks and acting with courage, exciting things can happen.

The same church I discussed earlier has another site they took over from a church that needed to close. They assumed the debt that this church still had and began the process of discerning what to do with this site. A variety of efforts were attempted, but none of them stuck. They did develop an impressive community garden that produces thousands of pounds of produce every year, but they were committed to doing far more with this location. It had a great deal of property and a facility that could be reimagined for any number of things.

At one point, the leadership entered into conversations with an organization that rehabilitated women who had been rescued from sex trafficking. It was a very risky venture as this type of work comes with some serious safety concerns. Sex traffickers don't take lightly to their women being rescued out of their system and will do whatever it takes to get those women back. High levels of security and secrecy were necessary.

The conversation progressed to the point of having neighborhood meetings to inform them of what was being considered for this campus. Eventually, they were granted a meeting with the city council to seek approval. At that meeting, hundreds of the city's residents showed up to vehemently oppose this church's desire to bring this organization onto that property as there was no way they wanted this type of organization putting their community at risk. By this time, the leadership of the congregation had been working for nearly two years to get to this point. At the end of the meeting, the city council denied their request and the project was squashed.

Like the stealing of a hundred apple trees, this could have been a moment of defeat. The congregation had tried a number of ideas and all of them had failed or lacked real impact. But not for this congregation. They have a leadership system, both lay and clergy, that has incredible resilience. Instead of seeing this as a defeat, they saw it as another learning moment to help guide them in discovering what could be possible on this site. They are ten years into this location and have yet to fully realize its purpose. The community garden continues to be successful but they are not going to settle there. People matter. This location has real possibility, and when that new possibility presents itself, they will act.

At the writing of this book, the congregation is now in serious conversation with a developer who wants to partner with them to explore some multi-use opportunities for this location. This time it feels right. In spite of years of push back and underperforming ventures, they are finally going to fully live into their mission at this location. Resilient leadership matters!

Failure is NOT Failure

Thomas Edison once said, "I have not failed. I have just found 10,000 ways that won't work."

When we first launched the assessment tool we use with churches called The Missional Assessment Profile (MAP), we had a statement that read, "This congregation is willing to fail when implementing changes." Our intention was to use this as a way to teach congregational leaders that failure is not a measure of weakness but an opportunity to learn and grow. After two years of using this tool, the pushback was so great on the use of the word "fail" that we finally gave in. There were too many clients that simply felt the word fail was a set-up for negativity and defeat. We didn't agree, but our team decided it wasn't worth pushing. Now, instead of the word fail, we frame the statement this way; "Our congregation is willing to take risks in order to fulfill its mission." It isn't nearly as strong as using the word fail, but it at least gives our consultants the opportunity to speak to the fact that risks do come with the potential of being wrong and can result in experiencing failure. AND, that is okay.

The point is fairly simple: If we are not willing to experience failure as we work towards meaningful change, we will never fully realize or experience what this new way of church can be. The light bulb was not discovered on the first attempt, or the second, or the 100th. Change requires resilient leadership who will keep at it and persevere. Resilient leadership does not see failure as a weakness but as a moment of discovery.

My preferred image for this complex and challenging time is that of an explorer. Most explorers don't launch their adventures with all the answers in place. They launch their adventures with the drive to discover. They know there is something to be found, but don't know exactly what that will be. That is the lure, the thing that makes it so intoxicating. Explorers are also acutely aware that there will be some missteps along the way, but those moments cannot become deterrents. Rather, those moments embolden them to keep pushing the mission forward.

One of the greatest examples of this is the story of Ernest Shackleton, the renowned polar explorer. He conducted three expeditions across the Antarctic. His third one was his most famous because it failed. The purpose of the mission, launched in 1914, was to traverse the Antarctic continent by dogsled via the south pole. He assembled a crew of 27 men and set sail on the ship Endurance to reach their intended landing point. Two months into the expedition, and about 60 nautical miles from their destination, the ship became frozen in the ice pack of the Weddell Sea. Now, instead of sailing, they were a prisoner of this ice pack and controlled by the ocean's currents.

After several months of being frozen in this ice pack and dragged by the ocean currents hundreds of miles away from their destination, it was apparent that not only was the expedition's intended purpose lost, the ship itself had to be abandoned. It was time to focus solely on survival. After nearly two years of living on ice flows, enduring brutal weather conditions, sailing on the most treacherous seas in the world in 22 ft. rescue boats, and traversing mountains that had never been climbed, the entire crew was saved. Not one death occurred during this incredible journey of endurance. It was ironic that the ship was named "Endurance".

Besides the feat of keeping every single member of the crew alive, there was another underlying mission in these brutal conditions. In order to secure financing for the expedition, Shackleton had sold the rights to all the photographs and film footage that would be taken during the adventure. One of the crew members, Frank Hurley, was an expert photographer and was tasked with visually documenting the journey. Incredibly, the entire journey of survival was captured by Hurley. In the middle of just trying to stay warm, find food, build shelters and sail treacherous seas, high quality photographs and film footage were taken at each stage. Shackleton never doubted that they would survive. He also knew that if he was going to be able to pay for this failed expedition, he would need those photographs and footage. It was a key priority to document the experience through those images.

Today, this failed expedition is one of the most famous. Ernest Shackleton is considered to be one of the most brilliant leaders of his time and his story is used as a framework for teaching characteristics of a highly effective leader. The photographs have become world renowned and are currently housed in the Royal Geographic Society in London, England. On a personal note, because of what this adventure symbolizes in regards to leadership and resilience, I have used some of the photographs as a branding image for a company I lead called The Leadership Laboratory.

Failure is not failure. It is opportunity to learn, to discover, to advance the adventure. Shackleton wanted to be the first person to traverse the Antarctic on dogsled via the south pole. But just as important, he wanted to document this adventure through film and photography. His failure to traverse the continent didn't lead to abandoning the mission, it simply took a different path that originally could never have been imagined.

This is how we should see this moment for the church. We are explorers on an adventure to discover what this world of church will look like into the future. Our failures in advancing the imagination of what this will be are not failures but lessons and opportunities to discover something new and different. We don't know what we don't know. So, let's start by taking actions to discover what we need to know and can learn from these moments. It will unfold in ways that we never could imagine. We will discover things we never envisioned. And although the future will look different than our past, we will indeed have a future.

Don't Think You are Immune to the Changes Around You

There are plenty of faith communities that have not been hit by these shifting sands. They have yet to experience a crisis of relevancy and impact. I am grateful for that but also very aware that this too shall pass. If these congregations don't engage in self-reflection and question their actions and behaviors, as well, the culture will catch up with them. If they are not prepared for it, they, too, will experience decline and marginalization. The globalization of culture and the pluralization of religion is real and continues to broaden in its affects. Simply because a church has found itself in a pocket of immunity right now doesn't mean that change isn't coming their way. For those churches lucky enough to be, as yet, unaffected, they should take this time of influence and relevance to become better prepared for the cultural shifts that will inevitably find their way into their neighborhood.

Words Matter

We are living in a time where words are becoming less and less reflective of the truth, especially when we hear things like, "alternative facts", "truth isn't always truth" or "it only matters what I can get you to believe, not what is actually true". I still want to hold out hope that words really do mean something, and mean what they say. Language is, after all, how we express our beliefs and value systems. Nothing will ever take the place of actions speaking louder than words, if our words don't reflect or support those actions, we are in trouble.

Over the past few years, it has become trendy for churches to put up signs on their properties trying to show support and love for their neighbors with different religious practices. "Blessed Ramadon" and "Happy Rosh Hashana!" are just two examples of what I have witnessed. I fully support this, however, I say to church leaders that if they put up these signs, it also means that they are stating that they respect and honor those religious practices as being legitimate. You can't put that sign on the outside of your church property and then inside your building say, "the only way to know God is to be baptized and accept Jesus as your only Lord and Savior." To be fair, you can say that, but then don't put those signs on your property. It isn't authentic to how you feel or how you believe.

It is important that we take the time to closely examine what we actually say when we gather as faith community. We have said things for so long that we have lost the ability to be objective and fully understand the affect. We no longer recognize what our words may be communicating. Every faith community has to grapple with their own belief system, and the words they feel are most important in articulating that belief. In doing so, these communities need to be very mindful of what their words are communicating and accept the consequences of those words. Don't be confused that people are put off by your faith community because you say you want to be fully inclusive and welcoming but your words don't match your actions. Don't get frustrated that people are not drawn to a culture whose words reflect that it's your way or the highway.

My hope is that your starting point in addressing the idea that words matter can be the very points I have tried to address with my own 'what if' questions. Do your words reflect that you actually believe your truth is the only truth? If so, is that really how you believe? If it is, then name it and accept the results when you do so. Do your words reflect a belief that your religious practice is the only right practice? If so, then accept the consequences of such words. Would you rather isolate yourselves verses collaborate? How do your words reflect either position? Do you love your neighbor in hopes of making them become like you? If that truly is what you believe, then own it and accept the consequences of such words and behavior. The point is, take seriously the need for your words to be fully aligned with your sense of mission and purpose.

In Closing

I don't believe that I am deluded enough to think I have all the answers or know exactly how this time needs to unfold. What I do believe is that avoiding the difficult questions will only delay, or prohibit, our potential in growing into a new way of being a church with impact and meaningful affect. I am confident in saying that if we keep acting, speaking and believing the way we have been, nothing will ultimately change. We have contributed to what is going on with the church in today's world. The only way I know how to move forward is for us to take a serious look at how we have contributed to our own condition. If we do this - and do this without fear and without envy - we can begin to think, act and believe differently. We can create a new day of joy and hopefulness. We can adapt and we can survive. I love my faith and I love my church. We have so much to offer. I am willing to pour my love into this transformation and I know that as faith communities, we can do this. Together, let's imagine a new church. It may look different than we thought and it may yet continue to change. But we don't need to be afraid. Let's launch ourselves into our own future and let us do it with love and vision.

ABOUT THE AUTHOR

JEFFREY KJELLBERG is the owner/president of three national faith based consulting firms that work to develop financial resources, create effective missional strategies, and equip vibrant leaders. Jeff served as a pastor in the ELCA for 15 years prior to becoming a consultant/owner. He has an undergraduate degree from Concordia College, Moorhead, MN (1983) and a M/Div. from Luther Seminary in St. Paul, MN (1983). Through his consulting work, Jeff has traveled the country engaging with thousands of leaders and hundreds of ministry contexts, giving him a wealth of insight and perspective to the current realities facing faith based communities. He has dedicated his career to helping these faith communities fully live into their holy purpose.

Jeff lives in St. Paul, MN with his wife, Melanie. They have four children and one grandchild. Jeff's passions are spending as much time with his family as possible, and traveling the world to experience the vast diversity of God's creation and the complexities and beauty of the human condition.

www.jeffreykjellberg.com